Cross-Stitch
A Beautiful Gift

Sharon Perna

Sterling Publishing Co., Inc.   New York

This book is dedicated to my father, Charles Lozier Perna, who encouraged me to oil-paint next to him as he worked on Westerns, made me a carpenter's tool box just like his, and sent me to college for two wonderful degrees in art.

Library of Congress Cataloging-in-Publication Data

Perna, Sharon.
    Cross-stitch a beautiful gift / Sharon Perna.
        p.   cm.
    Includes index.
    ISBN 0-8069-8400-7
    1. Cross-stitch—Patterns.   I. Title
    TT778.C76P423   1992
    746.44'3041—dc20   91-41489
                                     CIP

10 9 8 7 6 5 4 3 2 1

Published in 1992 by Sterling Publishing Company, Inc.
387 Park Avenue South, New York, N.Y. 10016
© 1992 by Sharon Perna
Distributed in Canada by Sterling Publishing
℅ Canadian Manda Group, P.O. Box 920, Station U
Toronto, Ontario, Canada M8Z 5P9
Distributed in Great Britain and Europe by Cassell PLC
Villiers House, 41/47 Strand, London WC2N 5JE, England
Distributed in Australia by Capricorn Link Ltd.
P.O. Box 665, Lane Cove, NSW 2066
Manufactured in the United States of America
All rights reserved

Sterling ISBN 0-8069-8400-7

CONTENTS

Color sections follow pages 32 and 96.

INTRODUCTION

In *Cross-Stitch a Beautiful Gift,* I had three goals in mind. First, I wanted to make a collection of forty-two cross-stitch projects that represented gifts you could make for a variety of different people and occasions. Second, I wanted the artwork, spanning a range from simple to challenging, to incorporate a wide variety of motifs, colors, thread counts, and supporting background materials. And finally, I wanted to group the gifts into six basic categories. These divisions, and their brief accompanying descriptions, are listed below.

In the first section entitled "Christmas Gifts," there are seven items to make the home more festive during this joyous holy season. The projects here decorate the Christmas tree, the dining table, the fireplace mantel, gift packages, and even the holiday host.

In the segment called "Valentine's Day Gifts," five presents enhance the table or the plants placed on it. For the table itself, there are articles like a place mat, runner, and card. And to enhance any potted greenery, there is a plant tub or plant pokes, which express several typical but short Valentine's Day messages.

The "Gifts for Family and Friends" category offers nine assorted projects. Included here are gifts for a birthday, Father's Day, to celebrate a new house, to serve as a going away present, or just to say thank you for favors done by family, neighbors, and friends. Often these items are placed in the space of a commercially made cross-stitch product or combined with a ready-made object like a frame, plaque, basket, or tote.

In the fourth subdivision called "Baby Gifts," seven patterns mix bright and pastel animals with colorful trims and words. Wishing only the best for the new baby or grandchild, these designs are simple and bold like those from a coloring book.

"Gifts for the Cat Fancier" is category five. In this section there are eight items that the cat admirer can use to proclaim an interest in felines of all kinds. Many of these articles are personal in nature; things like a bookmark, a box or tray for the dressing table, a notebook cover, or a pencil and pad container for telephone messages.

And finally, in "Heirloom Gifts," there are six items that the recipient can proudly display as the result of a very special birthday, graduation, wedding, or anniversary. These are the challenging projects involving lots of time and made with love. Worthy of being passed through the family as needlework treasures, these are the designs that remind us of important personal milestones long after the events have come and gone.

MATERIALS AND TECHNIQUES

MATERIALS

The Fabrics and Papers

The cross-stitching in this book is done on an evenweave fabric of cotton or a specially perforated paper for needlework. "Evenweave" means that the fabric is evenly woven so that it has the same number of threads to the inch in both directions of the cloth (horizontally and vertically). Just as the textile you will cross-stitch has a natural woven grid made by the crossing of the threads, the charted graph you will work from also has a corresponding framework which matches it perfectly.

Aida is a 100% cotton fabric available in white, ivory, solid colors, and in multicolor combinations. It is usually sold in pre-cut pieces or by the yard. The count of this fabric, that is, the number of cross-stitches you can sew in a one-inch space, is either 6, 8 (Illus. 1), 11, 14, or 18. You should also understand that the fabric count can be expressed in several different ways, but the interpretation is always the same. For example, #8 Aida, Aida 8, 8-count Aida cloth, and 8/1″ all mean that you can embroider 8 cross-stitches per inch on that particular fabric. If a project calls for a specific count, using another count only alters and distorts the final appearance of the design.

There are two things you need to learn about evenweave fabrics: The cotton is never preshrunk, and the cloth frays easily. The first statement is just a peculiarity in the way this cloth is handled. The fraying, however, can be managed in the following manner. Turn under ¼″ on the raw edges of the cotton. Press this measurement towards the wrong side of the cloth. Then finish off the raw edges by either: Machine-stitching twice ⅛″ from the edges (Illus. 2); whipping around the margins with a knotted double strand of thread (Illus. 3); or machine zigzag-stitching twice around the piece (Illus. 4).

Perforated paper for needlework can be purchased in needlecraft, craft shops, and through the buyers' guides of many craft oriented magazines. It is available in white or ivory, and it is sold in sheets that measure 9″ × 12″ each.

Perforated paper has a thread count of 14. And like a 14-count Aida cloth, two strands of embroidery floss are used for cross- and backstitching. Because the holes in this lightweight cardboard are very pronounced, a threaded needle slips easily through as you sew.

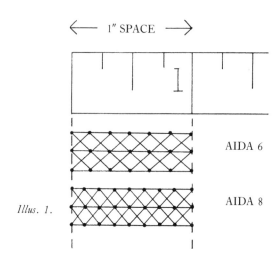

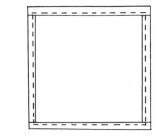

AIDA 6

AIDA 8

Illus. 1.

WRONG SIDE OF CLOTH

Illus. 2.

WRONG SIDE OF CLOTH   WRONG SIDE OF CLOTH

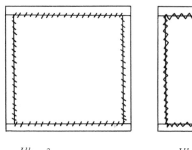

Illus. 3.   *Illus. 4.*

Threads and Needles

In each cross-stitch key, two brands of six-strand cotton embroidery floss are given. The J. & P. Coats wound embroidery floss is listed first because that is what I use. Other embroiderers are die-hard DMC fans (their floss is also referred to as mouliné spécial), so I have included their preference too. Since both brands are excellent, choose the floss you prefer or the one which is easiest to get locally.

Embroidery floss is marketed in skeins of approximately nine yards each. You can use all six strands of the thread or separate it into one, two, or possibly three strands cut into 14″ lengths. Since my artwork features perforated paper and cotton fabrics in a variety of counts, refer to each cross-stitch key for the specific thread requirements on that project.

Tapestry needles have blunt points, and they vary in size from #13 (the largest and heaviest) to #26 (the smallest and lightest). For all of the embroidery in this collection, use a #24 needle.

Miscellaneous Supplies

Cross-stitching is such a simple craft. When you have an evenweave material, some embroidery floss, scissors, and a tapestry needle, you really have all the sewing essentials that you need. However, the following supplies are also useful:

Thimble.
Threads. For general sewing use cotton-covered (wrapped) polyester.
Rulers. A 12- or 18-inch transparent plastic ruler is especially helpful.
Embroidery Hoops. Hoops are not necessary.
Tracing Paper. Sold in pads or in rolls, the light and medium weights are good for pattern-making.
Graph Paper. This is needed to work out the information, for example, that changes in the "Orange Calf" pillow. It is sold in needlecraft shops, office, drafting, and architectural supply stores. The erasable sheets with a grid of 8 (squares) × 8 (squares) to one inch are what I use and prefer.

100% Pure Poly-fil Fibre. Poly-fil fibre comes in a 12-ounce bag. It is washable, pulls apart easily, and can be used to stuff things such as the "Rabbit" door sign and the "Orange Calf" pillow insert.

Dressmaker's Tracing Paper (Washable and Dry Cleanable). Dressmaker's tracing paper is used to transfer pattern markings to either the right or wrong side of a fabric. Although each packet contains an assortment of coated colored papers, use white whenever it is possible. The white markings disappear easily from either the heat of an iron or from washing. For light- and medium-colored fabrics, select the lightest possible color of dressmaker's tracing paper.

To mark a fabric always place the waxy side of the paper next to the cloth that is to be inscribed. Then lightly trace over the markings in the pattern with a sewing gadget called a tracing wheel (Illus. 5).

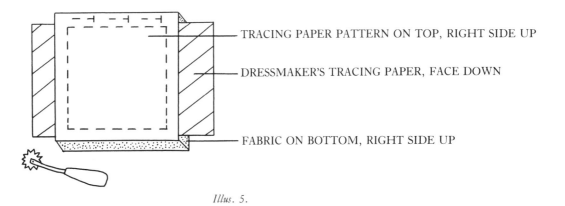

TRACING PAPER PATTERN ON TOP, RIGHT SIDE UP

DRESSMAKER'S TRACING PAPER, FACE DOWN

FABRIC ON BOTTOM, RIGHT SIDE UP

Illus. 5.

THE STITCHING TECHNIQUES

All the designs in this book are made with cross-stitches alone or cross-stitches in combination with backstitches. Both stitches are simple to make and easy to master.

Cross-Stitching on Cotton and Perforated Paper

Cross-stitches are worked by passing a blunt tapestry needle through the holes in a gridlike material. A completed cross-stitch is made in two movements: A left-to-right bottom stitch which slants like this / and a right-to-left top-stitch which slants like\. The cross-stitches that result can be made singly (Illus. 6) or embroidered in rows where the under-stitches are made in one direction, and the returns are worked in the opposite way (Illus. 7). Cross-stitches can also be sewn in horizontal, vertical, and diagonal directions. The rules state: All the stitches must be crossed in the same direction, and you make one cross-stitch within one square on an even-weave cotton or perforated paper (Illus. 8).

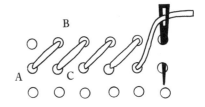

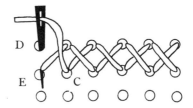

Illus. 7.
Rows of cross-stitches.
a. Work first strokes left to right. Bring needle up through hole in fabric at A. Insert thread diagonally across at B and come up at C. Pull thread through. Continue to end of row.
b. On return journey, complete other half of cross, sewing right to left. From C go over to D, then under and up to E (same hole as A).

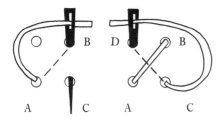

Illus. 6.
Single cross-stitch.
a. Bring needle up through hole in fabric at lower left corner of cross (A). Insert thread diagonally across at hole B and come up at C; Pull thread through.
b. Complete other half of cross; stitch from C to D.

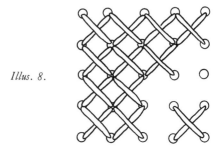

Illus. 8.

Backstitching on Cotton and Perforated Paper

Backstitches (Illus. 9) add detail to a surface that is predominantly filled with cross-stitches. Since they are used as accents, backstitches are worked after all the cross-stitching is complete. Like cross-stitches they can also be sewn horizontally, vertically, diagonally, or in line combinations. On an evenweave cotton or perforated paper, sew one backstitch within one square. On my charts, backstitches are indicated by a bold black line, and they are embroidered just as they appear on the charts.

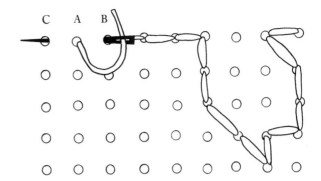

Illus. 9.
Backstitches.
a. All stitches are same size.
b. Work right to left even though stitches travel in different directions.
c. Bring needle up through hole in fabric at A.
d. Take small running stitch backwards to B and bring needle up in front of first stitch at C. Pull thread through.
e. Repeat taking another stitch backwards; put needle in same hole as A.

The Basic Sewing Procedures

UNDERSTANDING THE CHARTS

Cross-stitch designs are not printed on fabrics. You do the embroidery by counting from a graph or chart. As you would expect, the graphs vary in their complexity and the degree of work they require. Mine, for example, are divided into four categories that range from the simplest chart to the intermediate, advanced and most challenging.

As you look at each chart and work on the evenweave cotton or perforated paper, one square on the graph repre-sents one square on the cotton or perforated paper that can be filled with one cross-stitch. The different symbols in the design represent where a cross-stitch should be made and what color of floss needs to be used. Backstitches are indi-cated by a bold black line, and they are embroidered just as they appear on the charts. Plain squares are areas without embroidery.

Making the First Cross-Stitch

In the project sections of the book, you will repeatedly see the heading "Making the first cross-stitch." Very specific in-structions follow this phrase. For example, "Measure across 3¼" from top left corner; measure downwards 4" from top left corner. Mark point where two measurements intersect (Illus. 10). Refer to chart. Start sewing at arrow." If you follow these directions, you will usually be making your first cross-stitch at a spot on the fabric or paper (which corre-sponds to an arrow) which is almost always in the top left corner of the graph (Illus. 11). Refer to the cross-stitch key, and select the proper color of floss according to the symbols given. Then continue by making all the cross-stitches to the right and by sewing the rest of the design from left to right and from top to bottom.

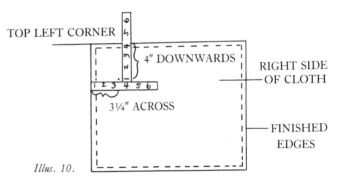

Illus. 10.

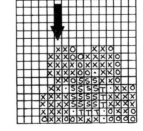

Illus. 11.

TOP LEFT CORNER OF GRAPH

Starting a Thread

After you have cut and separated the floss into the proper number of strands, do not knot the end. Leave, instead, a 1″ tail of floss hanging against the back of the material. Make your first cross-stitches as, at the same time, you secure the tail by working over it with the next few stitches (Illus. 12).

To begin a new thread after you have already worked several rows of embroidery, run your needle under four or five previously worked stitches on the reverse side of the material (Illus. 13). Then come up on the right side, and cross-stitch as usual.

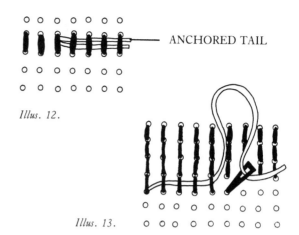

ANCHORED TAIL

Illus. 12.

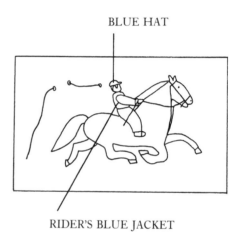

Illus. 13.

Carrying Threads

You do not have to finish off your embroidery floss when one color ends, if it will reappear in an adjacent area, and if the thread can be run under previous stitches. If, for example, you are sewing a blue hat, and the color reintroduces itself ¾″ away in a rider's jacket; do not end the color at the hat. Instead, carry the floss to an out-of-the-way place on the cloth or paper, come up on the right side of the material, take one long running stitch, come up, and then let the thread dangle until it is needed again (Illus. 14). At that point in time, rethread it, slide your needle under the previous stitches on the wrong side of the material, and travel to the new location. Continue sewing as usual. The one exception to this principle involves wide-open spaces. Try to avoid carrying a thread across an opening of ⅝″ or more. Loose unsupported threads can show through the front of an article, and they detract from the beauty of the design.

BLUE HAT

RIDER'S BLUE JACKET

Illus. 14.

Ending a Thread

To end a thread, slide your needle under four or five previous stitches on the back of the design and clip off the excess floss. Remember that the reverse side of the material should be as neat as the front. Therefore, no hanging threads.

Washing and Ironing Techniques

Once the cross-stitching on the fabric is done, the cloth needs to be hand- or machine-washed before you can proceed to the "Finishing directions." Even if the needlework appears clean, launder it anyway. This may be the last time that the piece is ever cleaned, and washing gives the fabric a nice neat look. To do this, use lukewarm water and a gentle soap.

With the iron set on cotton, press the embroidery on both sides. Then lay the article flat until it is thoroughly dried.

The Cross-Stitch Summary (Or How to Work a Project from Start to Finish)

Many of the cross-stitch procedures are repetitive; so I will list this information once. I am now, therefore, assuming that you are completing this basic routine unless stated otherwise in the "Finishing directions." The procedure goes like this:

1. Choose a design according to your sewing abilities. The heading (simple, intermediate, advanced, or challenging) indicates the degree of work required.

2. Refer to the project sections of this book. All the materials and the details for "Making the first cross-stitch" are presented here. Also glance through the "Finishing directions" just to make sure you understand how the item should be made from start to finish.

3. Do not preshrink evenweave cottons. Do not preshrink cording which will eventually be glued to an object. Do, however, preshrink any of the materials which will be used as linings, backings, or trims.

4. Cut your evenweave materials to the exact measurements given. Seam allowances are included within these dimensions. Evenweave fabrics fray. Finish off the raw edges by either hand- or machine-stitching (Illus. 2–4).

5. In the upper left corner of the fabric or perforated paper, find the starting point for the first cross-stitch (Illus. 10). On the charted design, this same reference point will be marked by an arrow (Illus. 11), which means start sewing here.

6. Do the embroidery by referring to the chart and cross-stitch key. Choose one brand from the two six-strand cotton embroidery flosses given. Then thread your needle with the correct number of strands that are listed in the cross- and backstitch keys. Use a #24 tapestry needle. For work on cotton and perforated paper, remember that one square on the graph represents one square on a material that can be filled with one complete cross-stitch. Backstitches are indicated by a bold black line, and they are embroidered just as they appear on the charts. Sew the cross-stitches first; add the backstitches later.

7. Wash the embroidered fabric. Press. Dry.

8. Go to the "Finishing directions."

9. Make all patterns that are required with tracing paper, pencil, and ruler.

10. To transfer any pattern markings to the right or wrong side of a fabric, always use the lightest possible color (white is preferable) of dressmaker's tracing paper and a tracing wheel (Illus. 5).

11. Remove any basting or running stitches that still show on the project.

12. In the diagrams which accompany this book, a (R) means that the fabric or paper is right side up; a (W) means it is wrong side up.

CHRISTMAS GIFTS

Toy Soldier *(In color on page C.) (Simple.)*

Size: Ornament approximately 2¾″ wide × 6⅜″.

Perforated paper, 14-count, ivory: Cut paper 3¾″ wide × 7″.

Embroidery floss: Coats 7161 Blue Lt. (or DMC 813), 3046 Christmas Red Bright (666), 8403 Black (310), 2307 Christmas Gold (783), 2293 Yellow Dark (743), 3067 Baby Pink (use Coats color), 1001 White (Snow-White), and 7023 Blue Med. (797). Purchase one skein of each.

Other materials: Gold felt, for backing, 3¾″ wide × 7″. Red satin ribbon, double-faced, ⅛″ wide × 8½″. Tracing paper. White glue.

Making the first cross-stitch: Measure across 1¾″ from top left corner; measure downwards ⅝″ from top left corner. Mark point where two measurements intersect. Refer to chart. Start sewing at arrow.

Finishing directions

1. With right sides up, place tracing paper over embroidery. Trace around outer edges of soldier. With pencil and ruler, measure ¼″ beyond all edges of design. Mark measurements with dots. Connect dots to form a solid outline (Illus 15).

Christmas tree ornament

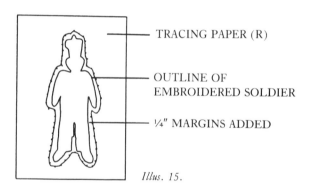

TRACING PAPER (R)

OUTLINE OF EMBROIDERED SOLDIER

¼″ MARGINS ADDED

Illus. 15.

2. With right sides up, place tracing paper pattern over felt. Pin. Cut out felt by cutting along solid outline.
3. With right sides up, trim perforated paper soldier to ⅛″ beyond edge of design.
4. Fold ribbon in half; get ends even. Crease middle. Place ends of ribbon ¾″ below plume in center of soldier's hat. Glue ribbon to back of perforated paper.
5. With right sides up, place felt flat. On back of perforated paper soldier, apply glue on edges of embroidery. Center soldier on top of felt (ends of ribbon are wedged in between) (Illus. 16). Gently squeeze two layers together. Put weight on top. Let dry.

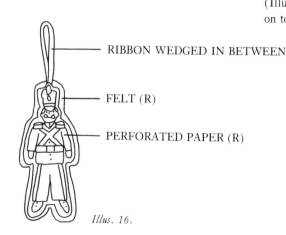

RIBBON WEDGED IN BETWEEN

FELT (R)

PERFORATED PAPER (R)

Illus. 16.

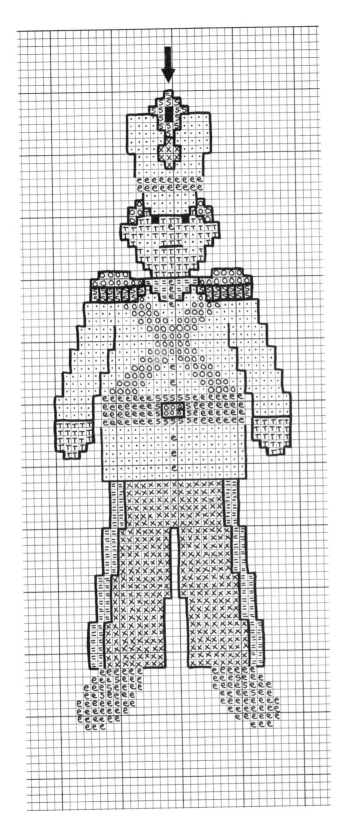

CROSS-STITCH KEY (use two strands)

Symbol	J. & P. Coats	DMC
■	7161 Blue Lt.	813
·	3046 Christmas Red Bright	666
e	8403 Black	310
s	2307 Christmas Gold	783
o	2293 Yellow Dark	743
T	3067 Baby Pink	Use J. & P. Coats color
=	1001 White	Snow-White
⊠	7023 Blue Med.	797
□	Paper as is	

BACKSTITCH KEY (use two strands)

Symbol	J. & P. Coats	DMC
	8403 Black	310

Backstitch Area: 8403 (or 310)—Everything.

Peace *(In color on page L.)* *(Simple.)*

Size: Embroidery approximately 2⅝" wide × 4¹¹⁄₁₆".

Perforated paper, 14-count, ivory: Cut paper 3⅞" wide × 5⅞".

Embroidery floss: Coats 7023 Blue Med. (or DMC 797), 1001 White (Snow-White), 3046 Christmas Red Bright (666), 3067 Baby Pink (use Coats color), 5000 Russet (434), and 8403 Black (310). Purchase one skein of each. Buy one spool Talon's gold metallic thread.

Other materials: Ivory card and matching envelope by Yarn Tree Designs of Ames, Iowa (card with design area of

Christmas card

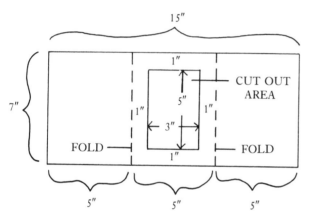

Illus. 17.

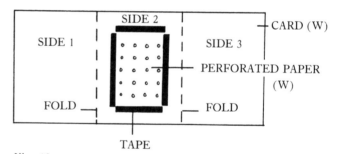

Illus. 18.

3" wide × 5", outer dimensions of 5" wide × 7" (Illus. 17)). Transparent tape, ¾" wide.

Making the first cross-stitch: Measure across ⅝" from top left corner; measure downwards ⅝" from top left corner. Mark point where two measurements intersect. Refer to chart. Start sewing at arrow.

Finishing directions

1. With right sides up, open card horizontally and center over embroidery. Use holes in perforated paper to help straighten design, to get margins equal at sides, and then top and bottom.

2. Turn card and embroidery over to wrong side. With four small pieces of tape, temporarily position angels in card. Check front to see that margins are still equal.

3. On back of perforated paper, permanently tape sides, top, and bottom to card. Do not allow tape to show through front of design (Illus. 18).

4. From extended position of card, fold side one over side two, covering back of embroidery. Write message on side three (Illus. 19).

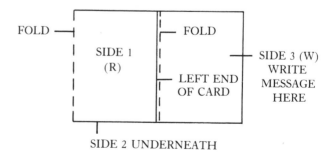

Illus. 19.

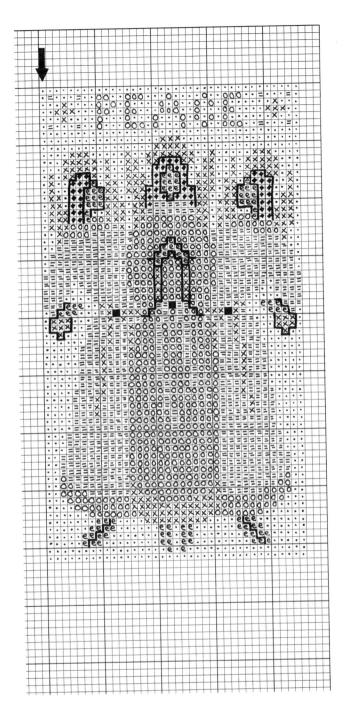

CROSS-STITCH KEY (use two strands)

Symbol	J. & P. Coats	DMC
·	7023 Blue Med.	797
o	1001 White	Snow-White
=	3046 Christmas Red Bright	666
e	3067 Baby Pink	Use J. & P. Coats color
◆	5000 Russet	434
■	8403 Black	310
□	Paper as is	

OTHER ITEM IN CROSS-STITCH KEY
(use three strands)

Symbol	Talon
⊠	Gold metallic thread from Talon

BACKSTITCH KEY (use two strands)

Symbol	J. & P. Coats	DMC
	8403 Black	310

Backstitch Area: 8403 Black (or 310)—Everything.

Basket Set *(In color on page B.)* *(Simple.)*

Size: Tags each approximately 3⅝″ wide × 3¾″.

Perforated paper, 14-count, ivory: Cut each paper 4¼″ wide × 4½″.

Embroidery floss: Coats 3046 Christmas Red Bright (or DMC 666), 6228 Christmas Green (909), 5471 Coffee Brown (433), and 7030 Blue (799). Purchase one skein of each. Buy one spool DMC's gold metallic thread (A broder, 72% viscose, 28% polyester, 40m).

Other materials: White construction paper, one sheet. Waterproof markers, red or green. White glue.

Making the first cross-stitch: For each tag measure across ⅝″ from top left corner; measure downwards ⅝″ from top left corner. Mark point where two measurements intersect. Refer to chart. Start sewing at arrow.

Finishing directions

1. On one gift tag, measure inside of top blank opening (Illus. 20). Reduce this measurement by ⅛″ on each side. Cut three pieces construction paper same size. With marker write holiday message (Happy Holidays, Merry Christmas, or Season's Greetings), recipient's name, complimentary close (Sincerely, Cordially, Affectionately, or Love), and your name. Center each line (Illus. 21).

2. On back of construction paper, lightly apply glue in corners. With right sides up, center and press label in top portion of tag. Let dry.

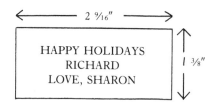

MEASURE HERE
(MINE MEASURED
2¹¹⁄₁₆″ WIDE × 1⅝″)

PERFORATED PAPER (R)

Illus. 20.

CONSTRUCTION PAPER (R)

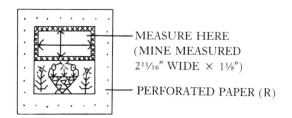

← 2 ⁹⁄₁₆″ →

HAPPY HOLIDAYS
RICHARD
LOVE, SHARON

↕ 1 ⅜″

Illus. 21.

3. On each tag add ¼″ margins beyond all four sides of embroidery. Use pencil and ruler. Cut off excess paper (Illus. 22).

Coordinated gift tags

Illus. 22.

¼″

PERFORATED PAPER (R)

¼″   ¼″ MARGINS

¼″

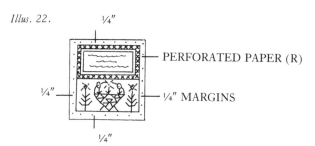

4. Add string to each tag. Cut one piece of red floss 10″ long. Separate floss into three groups of two strands each. Use one group per tag. Thread and knot as shown (Illus. 23 and 24).

5. Tags can later be used as Christmas tree ornaments.

TOP OF TAG DETAIL (R)

Illus. 23.

HAPPY HOLIDAYS
RICHARD
LOVE, SHARON

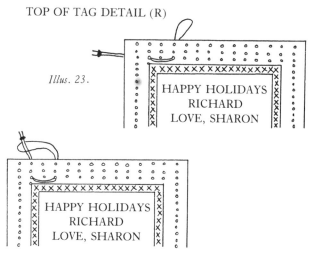

HAPPY HOLIDAYS
RICHARD
LOVE, SHARON

Illus. 24.

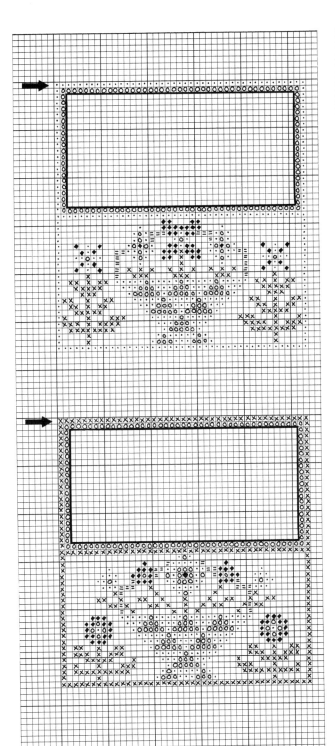

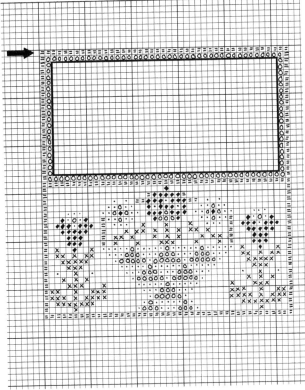

CROSS-STITCH KEY (use two strands)

Symbol	J. & P. Coats	DMC
·	3046 Christmas Red Bright	666
⊠	6228 Christmas Green	909
⊟	5471 Coffee Brown	433
◆	7030 Blue	799
☐	Paper as is	

OTHER ITEM IN CROSS-STITCH KEY
(use three strands)

Symbol		
⊡	Gold metallic thread from DMC	

BACKSTITCH KEY

Symbol	J. & P. Coats	DMC
	3046 Christmas Red Bright	666
	6228 Christmas Green	909
	5471 Coffee Brown	433

Backstitch Area: 3046 Christmas Red Bright (or 666)—Outline on red tag. 6228 Christmas Green (909)—Outline on green tag. 5471 Coffee Brown (433)—Outline on brown tag.

Snowman Set *(In color on page L.) (Simple.)*

Coordinated place mat and napkin

Size: Embroidery on place mat approximately 4" wide × 6⅛". Embroidery on napkin approximately 3¼" wide × 2".

Aida 14, red: Cut place mat 18" wide × 12". Cut napkin 14" wide × 12".

Embroidery floss: Coats 1001 White (or DMC Snow-White), 7001 Peacock Blue (use Coats color), 2314 Tangerine Med. (741), 3046 Christmas Red Bright (666), 8403 Black (310), 6001 Parrot Green Lt. (907), and 6227 Christmas Green Bright (700). Purchase one skein of each for set.

Making the first cross-stitch: See Steps 4 and 5.

Finishing directions

1. Fringe place mat and napkin before doing embroidery. To do, first measure ¾" from edges of each fabric. Mark cloth with pins. Using knotted single strand of red thread, connect and hand-stitch these lines by following one row in Aida and by weaving in and out cloth with ½" running stitches, pivoting at corners (Illus. 25 and 26).

PLACE MAT (R)

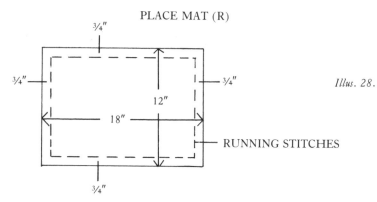

RUNNING STITCHES

Illus. 25.

2. With red thread and sewing machine set for satin stitching (⅛" side), stitch once around place mat and napkin, pivoting at corners. Sew right over ½" running stitches. Start in middle of bottom (Illus. 27).

PLACE MAT (R)

Illus. 27.

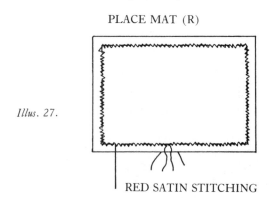

RED SATIN STITCHING

3. Using big heavy needle, fringe place mat and napkin up to satin stitching. Starting at edges of each fabric and working towards machine-stitching, pull out threads one at a time. Do sides first, then top and bottom (Illus. 28).

PLACE MAT (R)

Illus. 28.

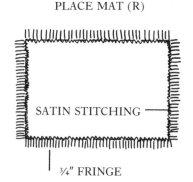

SATIN STITCHING

¾" FRINGE

4. On place mat, locate first cross-stitch. With right sides up and working in top left corner, count in margin of five squares from satin stitching at top and side. Mark cloth with pins. Using knotted single strand of thread, connect and

NAPKIN (R)

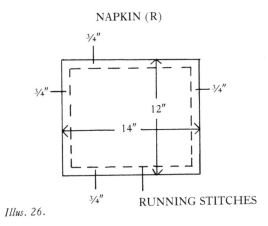

Illus. 26.

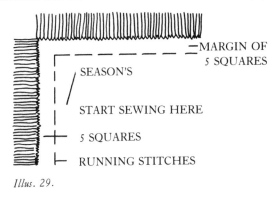

Illus. 29.

hand-stitch these two lines by following one row in Aida and by weaving in and out cloth with ½" running stitches. These lines now block out top and left edges of area to be embroidered (Illus. 29). Refer to chart. Start sewing at arrow.

5. On napkin, locate first cross-stitch. With right sides up, fold napkin vertically into three equal segments (fringe included). Mark two folds with pins. This design is 45 stitches wide and 28 stitches high. Count horizontal squares between two marked folds. Subtract 45 stitches from your figure. Divide unused squares by two. Center your design by using these numbers (mine were ten squares) as your side margins.

Mark cloth with pins. Next, at bottom of napkin, count up ten squares from satin stitching. Mark cloth with pin. From pin, count up an additional 28 squares. Mark end of last square with pin. With pins as your guide, block out area to be embroidered. Using knotted single strand of thread, connect and hand-stitch these lines by following one row in Aida and by weaving in and out cloth with ½" running stitches (Illus. 30). Refer to chart. Start sewing at arrow.

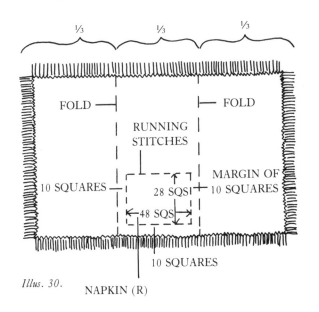

Illus. 30.   NAPKIN (R)

Chart and Cross-Stitch Key on following page.

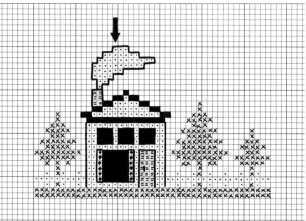

CROSS-STITCH KEY (use two strands)

Symbol	J. & P. Coats	DMC
·	1001 White	Snow-White
◆	7001 Peacock Blue	Use J. & P. Coats color
=	2314 Tangerine Med.	741
○	3046 Christmas Red Bright	666
■	8403 Black	310
♥	6001 Parrot Green Lt.	907
⊠	6227 Christmas Green Bright	700
☐	Cloth as is	

BACKSTITCH KEY (use two strands)

Symbol	J. & P. Coats	DMC
	8403 Black	310

Backstitch Area: 8403 Black (or 310)—Everything.

Striped Stocking *(In color on page C.)* *(Simple.)*

Size: Ornament approximately 4″ wide × 6″.

Perforated paper, 14-count, ivory: Cut paper 5″ wide × 7″.

Embroidery floss: Coats 6258 Willow Green (or DMC 987), 1001 White (Snow-White), 2307 Christmas Gold (783), 3151 Cranberry Very Lt. (604), 3046 Christmas Red Bright (666), 8403 Black (310), 7161 Blue Lt. (813), 7023 Blue Med. (797), 6238 Chartreuse Bright (use Coats color), 2293 Yellow Dark (743), 3067 Baby Pink (use Coats color). Purchase one skein of each.

Other materials: Gold felt, for backing, 5″ wide × 7″. Red satin ribbon, double-faced, ⅛″ wide × 8½″. Five silver bells, each ⁷⁄₁₆″ in diameter. Tracing paper. White glue.

Making the first cross-stitch: Measure across 2³⁄₁₆″ from top left corner; measure downwards ⅝″ from top left corner. Mark point where two measurements intersect. Refer to chart. Start sewing at arrow.

Christmas tree ornament

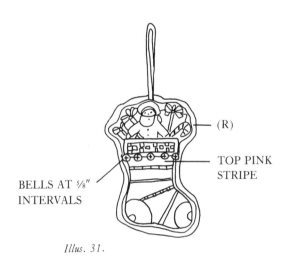

(R)

TOP PINK STRIPE

BELLS AT ⅝″ INTERVALS

Illus. 31.

Finishing directions

1. Repeat Steps 1–5 in "Toy Soldier." The only exception is: At Step 4 place ends of ribbon behind Santa's hat.
2. Add bells to top pink stripe in stocking. Using two strands knotted pink floss, attach bells at ⅝″ intervals. Starting at back of felt, come up through perforated paper. String on bell. Go down through felt. Come up again ⅝″ to right. Repeat (Illus. 31). Knot on back of fabric.

CROSS-STITCH KEY (use two strands)

Symbol	J. & P. Coats	DMC
▢	6258 Willow Green	987
△	1001 White	Snow-White
⊟	2307 Christmas Gold	783
⊡	3151 Cranberry Very Lt.	604
⊠	3046 Christmas Red Bright	666
■	8403 Black	310
▲	7161 Blue Lt.	813
s	7023 Blue Med.	797
e	6238 Chartreuse Bright	Use J. & P. Coats color
T	2293 Yellow Dark	743
U	3067 Baby Pink	Use J. & P. Coats color
▢	Paper as is	

BACKSTITCH KEY (use two strands)

Symbol	J. & P. Coats	DMC
	8403 Black	310

Backstitch Area: 8403 Black (or 310)—Everything.

Chart on following page.

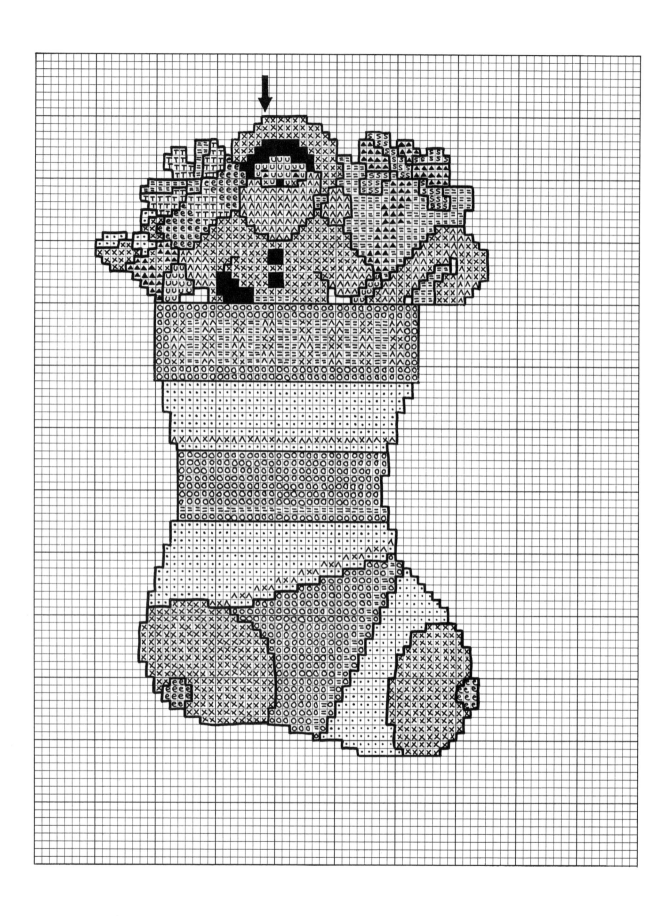

Candles in Repeat *(In color on page B.)* *(Intermediate.)*

Christmas card holder

Size: Embroidery approximately 9¼" wide × 3³⁄₁₆".

Aida 14, red: Cut cloth 11¾" wide × 5¾".

Embroidery floss: Coats 8403 Black (or DMC 310), 3046 Christmas Red Bright (666), 6227 Christmas Green Bright (700), and 1001 White (Snow-White). Purchase one skein of each. Buy one spool DMC's gold metallic thread (A broder, 72% viscose, 28% polyester, 40m).

Other materials: Rectangular basket, 11½" wide × 5" high × 8½" deep (Illus. 32). Black maxi piping, ⅞ yard. Lightweight cardboard, 10" wide × 4". White glue.

BASKET

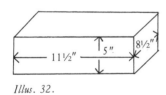

Illus. 32.

Making the first cross-stitch: Measure across 1¼" from top left corner; measure downwards 1¼" from top left corner. Mark point where two measurements intersect. Refer to chart. Start sewing at arrow.

Finishing directions

1. On each side of design, add margin of three squares of Aida beyond gold backstitches. Mark cloth with pins. Using knotted single strand of thread, connect and hand-stitch these lines by following one row in Aida and by weaving in and out cloth with ½" running stitches. These stitched lines are now new edges of needlework (Illus. 33).

AIDA (R)

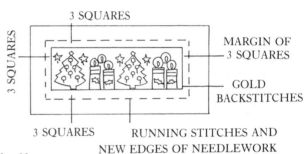

Illus. 33.

2. On running stitches press back sides of cloth. Press back top and bottom (Illus. 34).

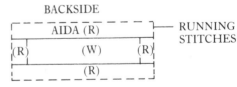

Illus. 34.

3. With wrong sides up, baste piping on Aida. Begin in middle of bottom. Turn ends upward at start and finish. Arrange so folded edges of piping face out and commercial stitching on piping rests on and is hidden by folded edges of fabric. Overlap ends by 1¼" (Illus. 35).

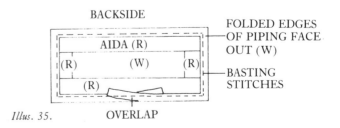

Illus. 35.

Chart and Cross-Stitch Key on following pages.

4. With right sides up, machine-stitch piping to Aida. Stitch close to folded edges of fabric, pivoting at corners (Illus. 36). Use red thread.

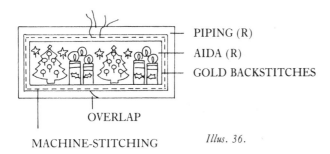

PIPING (R)
AIDA (R)
GOLD BACKSTITCHES

OVERLAP

MACHINE-STITCHING

Illus. 36.

5. Tuck cardboard inside back of design to add body and give it weight (Illus. 37).

6. Apply glue to back of design along edges of piping. With right sides up, center Aida/cardboard on basket. As glue hardens, keep pressing cloth to basket. Let dry.

BACKSIDE

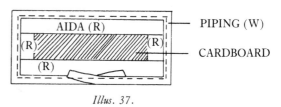

AIDA (R)
(R)
(R)
(R)

PIPING (W)

CARDBOARD

Illus. 37.

BACKSTITCH KEY (use two strands)

Symbol	J. & P. Coats	DMC
	8403 Black	*310*

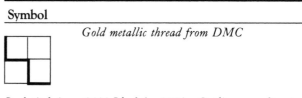

CROSS-STITCH KEY (use two strands)

Symbol	J. & P. Coats	DMC
⊠	*8403 Black*	*310*
◆	*3046 Christmas Red Bright*	*666*
·	*6227 Christmas Green Bright*	*700*
⊟	*1001 White*	*Snow-White*
☐	*Cloth as is*	

OTHER ITEM IN CROSS-STITCH KEY
(use one strand)

Symbol	
⊡	*Gold metallic thread from DMC*

OTHER ITEM IN BACKSTITCH KEY
(use one strand)

Symbol	
	Gold metallic thread from DMC

Backstitch Area: 8403 Black (or 310)—Outline around top tree ornament and outline around candles. Gold metallic thread—Outline around black rectangular border.

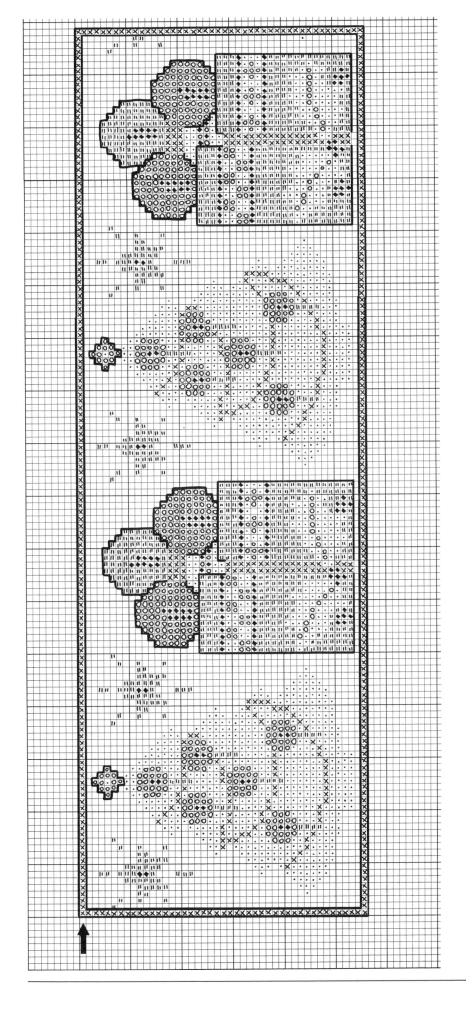

Holly Set *(In color on page C.) (Intermediate.)*

Coordinated apron pocket and chef's cap

Size. Pocket band approximately 6 1/16″ wide × 1 7/8″. Cap band approximately 19 1/4″ wide × 1 7/8″ without edging.

Maxi-weave Ribband, 14-count, white with gold edging, 1 7/8″ wide: Cut band 9″ for pocket. Cut band 22 1/2″ for hat. Purchase 7/8 yard for set.

Embroidery floss: Coats 3046 Christmas Red Bright (or DMC 666), 5363 Old Gold Lt. (use Coats color), 3021 Christmas Red Dk. (498), 8403 Black (310), use DMC color (369), and 6205 Emerald Green Med. (911). Purchase two skeins each of 5363 Old Gold Lt. (use Coats color) and 6205 Emerald Green Med. (911). Buy one skein of each remaining color for set.

Other materials: Red butcher's apron, 50% polyester and 50% cotton, one size fits all, pocket 6 5/8″ wide × 6 3/4″. White chef's cap, 100% cotton, one size fits all, rim 24″ around × 3 1/2″ with 4 1/2″ elasticized section in back (Illus. 38). White pregathered cotton eyelet edging, 1 1/8″ wide × 1 3/8 yards.

BACK OF CAP (R)

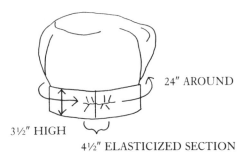

24″ AROUND

3 1/2″ HIGH

4 1/2″ ELASTICIZED SECTION

Illus. 38.

Making the first cross-stitch: For pocket, measure across 1 1/2″ from left end of horizontally held Ribband. For cap, measure across 1 5/8″ from left end of horizontally held Ribband. Refer to charts. Start sewing at arrows.

Finishing directions

1. Sew holly design once for apron.
2. Remove pocket from apron. With right sides up, center and place Ribband 7/8″ from top edge of pocket. Fold ends of Ribband back behind pocket. Press. Trim ends to 1″ beyond fold. Pin. Baste Ribband on pocket. Machine-stitch along top and bottom edges, sewing just inside gold edging (Illus. 39). Use white thread.

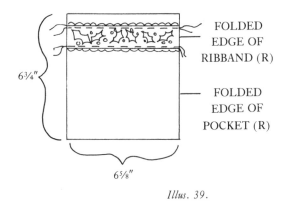

FOLDED EDGE OF RIBBAND (R)

FOLDED EDGE OF POCKET (R)

6 3/4″

6 5/8″

Illus. 39.

3. With right sides up, place pocket on apron in original position. Pin. Baste. Machine-stitch along sides and bottom edge of pocket, pivoting at corners (Illus. 40). Use red thread.

APRON (R)

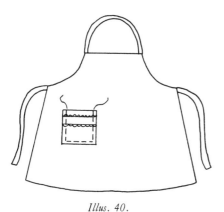

Illus. 40.

FOLDED EDGE OF
EYELET (R)

FOLDED EDGE OF
RIBBAND (R)

Illus. 42.

6. With right sides up, baste eyelet heading so it is hidden under top and bottom edges of Ribband. At start and finish of eyelet, remove ½″ heading but not eyelet. Then turn back ends by ¼″ (Illus. 42).

7. With right sides up, center Ribband/eyelet on rim, avoiding elasticized area at back. Pin. Baste. Machine-stitch along top, sides, and bottom edges, sewing just inside gold edging (Illus. 43). Use white thread.

4. For embroidery on cap, I had ten holly repeats which alternated from leaves up to leaves down. Each repeat has one square of Aida in between, and entire design is framed by two rows of gold cross-stitches. Design does not cross elasticized back of rim (Illus. 41). Since your cap may require fewer or more holly repeats, keep trying band on hat to see how many full repeats need to be sewn.

5. Fold ends of Ribband back ¼″ beyond gold cross-stitches. Press. Trim ends of Ribband to ¼″ beyond fold.

BACK OF CAP (R)

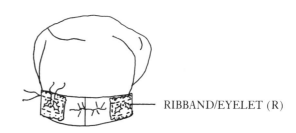

RIBBAND/EYELET (R)

Illus. 43.

BACK OF CAP (R)

ELASTICIZED BACK—NO RIBBAND HERE

Illus. 41.

CROSS-STITCH KEY (use two strands)

Symbol	J. & P. Coats	DMC
⊟	3046 Christmas Red Bright	666
⊠	5363 Old Gold Lt.	Use J. & P. Coats color
⊡	3021 Christmas Red Dk.	498
■	8403 Black	310
◆	Use DMC color	369
·	6205 Emerald Green Med.	911
☐	Cloth as is	

BACKSTITCH KEY (use two strands)

Symbol	J. & P. Coats	DMC
	8403 Black	310

Backstitch Area: 8403 Black (or 310)—Everything.

Chart on following page.

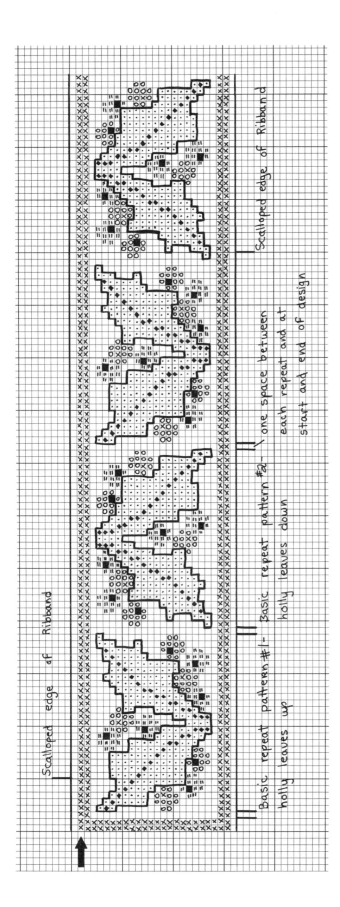

Scalloped edge of Ribband

Scalloped edge of Ribband

Basic repeat pattern #1- holly leaves up

Basic repeat pattern #2- one space between each repeat and at start and end of design holly leaves down

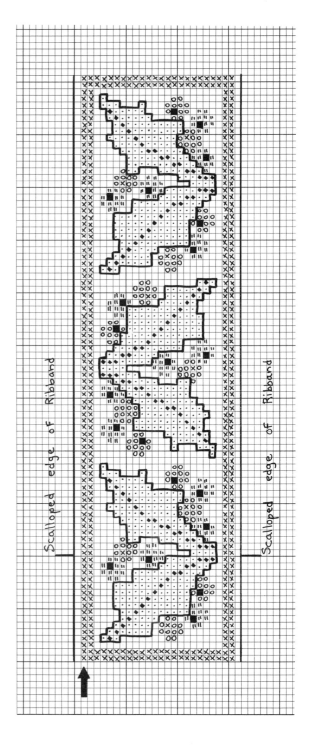

Scalloped edge of Ribband

Scalloped edge of Ribband

Top: "Tropical Fish" tote bag, page 54. Bottom: "Shells" tray, page 114.

"Basket Set," the three coordinated gift tags, is on page 20. The Christmas card holder, called "Candles in Repeat," is on page 27.

B

Clockwise: Christmas tree ornaments, "Striped Stocking" (page 25) and "Toy Soldier" (page 16), and coordinated apron pocket and chef's cap, "Holly Set" (page 30).

D

Facing page: coordinated wall hangings, "Hawaii One" and "Hawaii Two,"
page 118.

Above: "Daffodils" birthday plate, page 58.

ashley marie patterson
born on july 18, 1990
7 lbs. 4 ozs., 20 inches
greenwich, connecticut

Facing page: (top) "Orange Calf," birth announcement pillow, on page 78; (bottom, left to right) various bibs—"Bears" on page 70, "Owl" on page 74, "Blocks" on page 72, and "Ducks" on page 68.

Above: "Cyclamen" pillow on page 64; coordinated plant pokes, called "Clown Set," on page 40; and "Three Bushels in Repeat" basket band on page 48.

"Geometric Heart Set" coordinated towels, page 56.

VALENTINE'S
DAY
GIFTS

Interlocking Heart Set *(In color on page L.) (Simple.)*

Coordinated place mat and napkin

Size: Embroidery on place mat approximately 1⁹⁄₁₆″ wide × 8¹⁵⁄₁₆″. Embroidery on napkin approximately ¹³⁄₁₆″ wide × 4⁵⁄₁₆″.

Aida 14, white: Cut place mat 18″ wide × 12″. Cut napkin 12″ square.

Embroidery floss: Coats 7001 Peacock Blue (use Coats color), 3046 Christmas Red Bright (666), 3153 Geranium (956), 3021 Christmas Red Dk. (815), 3151 Cranberry Very Lt. (605), and use DMC color (3607). Purchase one skein of each for set.

Making the first cross-stitch: See Steps 2 and 3.

Finishing directions

1. Repeat Steps 1–3 in "Snowman Set." The only exceptions are: At Step 1, use white thread, and this napkin is square.
2. On place mat locate first cross-stitch. With right sides up and working in top left corner, count in margin of nine squares from satin stitching at top and side. Mark cloth with pins. Using knotted single strand of thread, connect and hand-stitch these two lines by following one row in Aida and by weaving in and out cloth with ½″ running stitches. These lines now block out top and left edges of area to be embroidered (Illus. 44). Refer to chart. Start sewing at arrow.

When embroidery is done, there should be a margin of nine or ten squares at bottom of design.

3. On napkin locate first cross-stitch. With right sides up and working in top right corner, count in margin of twelve squares fro⸱ satin stitching at side. Also count down seven squares from ⸱⸱in stitching at top. Mark cloth with pins. Block out top and right edges of area to be embroidered as in Step 2 (Illus. 45). Refer to chart. Start sewing at arrow.
4. Napkin and chart are intentionally turned upside down to make embroidering easier.
5. Fold napkin in quarters with hearts at left edge (Illus. 46).

PLACE MAT (R)

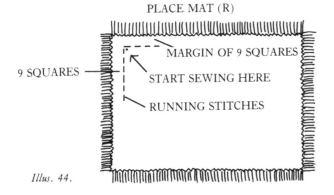

Illus. 44.

NAPKIN (R)

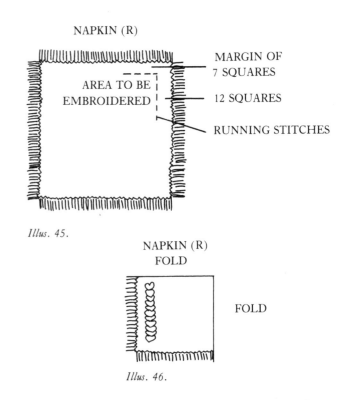

Illus. 45.

NAPKIN (R)
FOLD

FOLD

Illus. 46.

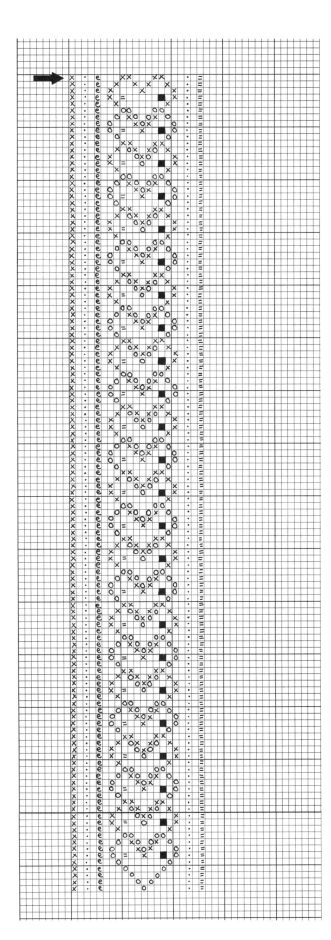

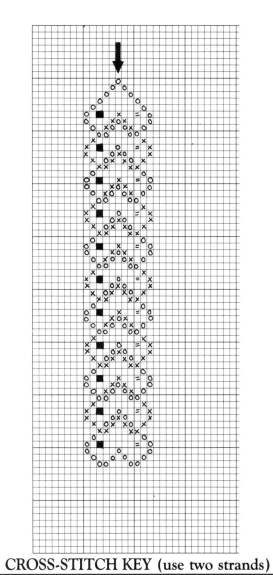

CROSS-STITCH KEY (use two strands)

Symbol	J. & P. Coats	DMC
■	*7001 Peacock Blue*	*Use J. & P. Coats color*
=	*3046 Christmas Red Bright*	*666*
·	*3153 Geranium*	*956*
⊠	*3021 Christmas Red Dk.*	*815*
⊡	*3151 Cranberry Very Lt.*	*605*
ⓔ	*Use DMC color*	*3607*
☐	*Cloth as is*	

Mirrored Hearts *(In color on page M.) (Simple.)*

Plant tub

Size: Embroidery approximately 12″ wide × 1⅞″.

Maxi-weave Ribband, 14-count, white with pink edging, 1⅞″ wide: Cut band ¾ yards.

Embroidery floss: Coats 6256 Parrot Green Med. (or DMC 906), 2293 Yellow Dark (743), 5470 no name (433), 3001 Cranberry Lt. (604), and 3046 Christmas Red Bright (666). Purchase one skein of each.

Other materials: Tub planter by Mill Store Products (unfinished wood ready to paint, 15″ wide × 8″ high × 5″ deep, with recessed design area measuring 15½″ wide × 1⅞″ (Illus. 47), style #0-650). White paint, 100% acrylic latex luster enamel. Brush, 100% polyester, 1½″ wide. Fine sandpaper.

FRONT

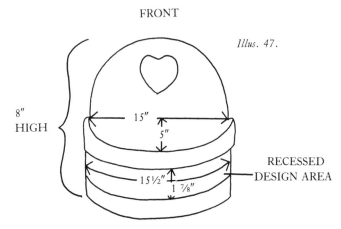

Illus. 47.

8″ HIGH

15″

5″

15½″ 1⅞″

RECESSED DESIGN AREA

Making the first cross-stitch: Measure across 5½″ from left end of horizontally held Ribband. See Step 1.

Finishing directions

1. This design has 12″ of embroidery, 1⅝″ of plain fabric showing on either side of hearts, and a lapover area in back. Make sure your planter can accommodate at least 12″ of embroidery even if side margins differ. Refer to chart. Start sewing at arrow.

2. Paint entire tub with three coats. Follow acrylic directions for painting, drying, sanding, and dusting after application of coats one and two.

3. With right sides up, center Ribband in recessed area of tub. Lap end over start. Slip-stitch or glue ends together (Illus. 48 and 49).

FRONT

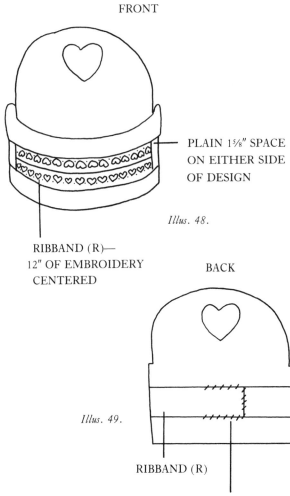

PLAIN 1⅝″ SPACE ON EITHER SIDE OF DESIGN

Illus. 48.

RIBBAND (R)— 12″ OF EMBROIDERY CENTERED

BACK

Illus. 49.

RIBBAND (R)

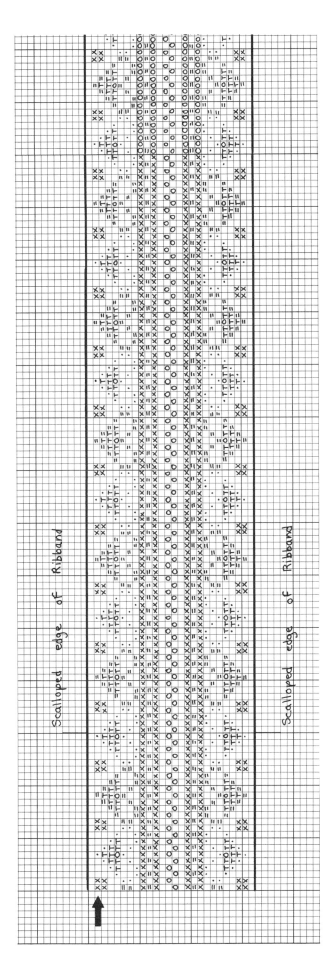

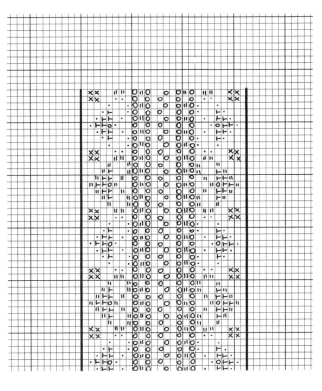

CROSS-STITCH KEY (use two strands)

Symbol	J. & P. Coats	DMC
⊡	6256 Parrot Green Med.	906
⊤	2293 Yellow Dark	743
·	5470 no name	433
⊠	3001 Cranberry Lt.	604
⊟	3046 Christmas Red Bright	666
☐	Cloth as is	

Dove *(In color on page L.)* *(Intermediate.)*

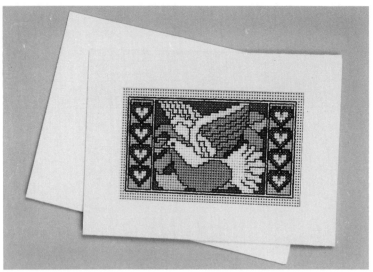

Valentine card

Size: Embroidery approximately 4⅝″ wide × 2 ⅝″.

Embroidery floss: Coats 7001 Peacock Blue (or DMC 996), 7159 Blue Very Lt. (827), 1001 White (Snow-White), 3126 Melon Lt. (3326), 3000 Garnet (815), 8900 Beaver Grey Med. (647), 3046 Christmas Red Bright (666), and 8403 Black (310). Purchase one skein of each.

Other materials: Ivory card and matching envelope by Yarn Tree Designs of Ames, Iowa (card with design area of 5″ wide × 3″, outer dimensions of 7″ wide × 5″ (Illus. 50)). Transparent tape, ¾″ wide.

Making the first cross-stitch: Measure across ¾″ from top left corner. Measure downwards ¾″ from top left corner. Mark point where two measurements intersect. Refer to chart. Start sewing at arrow.

Finishing directions

1. Repeat Steps 1–4 in "Peace." The only exceptions are: This card is held vertically, and at Step 4, refer to this diagram (Illus. 51).

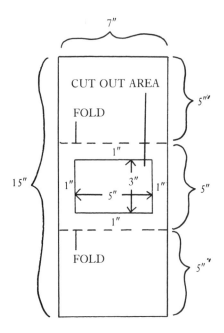

Illus. 50.

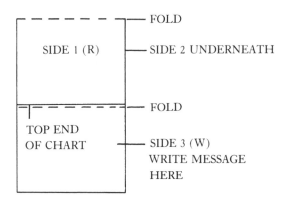

Illus. 51.

CROSS-STITCH KEY (use two strands)

Symbol	J. & P. Coats	DMC
⊠	7001 Peacock Blue	996
Ⓢ	7159 Blue Very Lt.	827
Ⓞ	1001 White	Snow-White
⊟	3126 Melon Lt.	3326
◆	3000 Garnet	815
ⓔ	8900 Beaver Grey Med.	647
·	3046 Christmas Red Bright	666
☐	Cloth as is	

BACKSTITCH KEY (use two strands)

Symbol	J. & P. Coats	DMC
	8403 Black	310

Backstitch Area: 8403 Black (or 310)—Everything.

Clown Set *(In color on page G.)* *(Intermediate.)*

Coordinated plant pokes

Size: Plant pokes each approximately 3½″ to 4¼″ wide × 5½″ to 5¾″.

Perforated paper, 14-count, ivory: Cut paper 5″ wide × 6″ for "Love Ya" and 4¼″ wide × 6¼″ each for "I Love You" and "Loving You."

Embroidery floss: Coats 3001 Cranberry Lt. (or DMC 604), 3046 Christmas Red Bright (666), 5470 no name (433), 6256 Parrot Green Med. (use Coats color), 6228 Christmas Green (699), 1001 White (Snow-White), 2314 Tangerine Med. (741), and 2293 Yellow Dark (743). Purchase two skeins each of 6256 Parrot Green Med. (use Coats color) and 2293 Yellow Dark (743). Buy one skein of each remaining color for set.

Other materials: Pink felt, for backing, 8¾″ wide × 12″. Red satin ribbon, double-faced, ⅛″ wide × 1½ yards. Three ting ting sticks, bamboo skewers, or wooden dowels, each ⅛″ to ³⁄₁₆″ wide × 13″. Tracing paper. White glue.

Making the first cross-stitch: For "Love Ya" measure across 2¼″ (for "I Love You" measure across 1½″, and for "Loving You" measure across 2³⁄₁₆″) from top left corner; on each measure downwards ⅝″ from top left corner. Mark point where two measurements intersect. Refer to charts. Start sewing at arrows.

Finishing directions

1. Repeat Steps 1–3 and 5 in "Toy Soldier." The only exception is: At Step 5 there is no ribbon wedged in between paper and felt.

2. Center and glue one stick to back of each clown. Glue stick ¼″ below top edge of felt. With embroidery face down, put weight on top and let dry.

3. Cut ribbon into three 18″ lengths. Tie one ribbon around one stick just beneath bottom of felt. Double knot.

CROSS-STITCH KEY (use two strands)

Symbol	J. & P. Coats	DMC
S	3001 Cranberry Lt.	604
◆	3046 Christmas Red Bright	666
◯	5470 no name	433
·	6256 Parrot Green Med.	Use J. & P. Coats color
3	6228 Christmas Green	699
L	1001 White	Snow-White
⊟	2314 Tangerine Med.	741
⊠	2293 Yellow Dark	743
☐	Paper as is	

BACKSTITCH KEY (use two strands)

Symbol	J. & P. Coats	DMC
	3046 Christmas Red Bright	666
	5470 no name	433

Backstitch Area: 3046 Christmas Red Bright (or 666)—Facial details and lettering within hearts. 5470 no name (433)— Everything else.

Hearts and Lilies *(In color on page N.)* *(Advanced.)*

Size: Embroidery contained on both ends in area approximately 9″ wide × 10″.

Aida 11, white: Cut cloth 15″ wide × 39″.

Embroidery floss: Coats 3150 Dusty Rose Very Lt. (or DMC 818), 3046 Christmas Red Bright (666), 2099 Pumpkin (971), 5471 Coffee Brown (433), 6020 Nile Green (954), 3128 Carnation Dk. (602), 6256 Parrot Green Med. (581), 6258 Willow Green (987), 7159 Blue Very Lt. (827), and 3000 Garnet (816). Purchase four skeins of Christmas Red Bright (666) and two skeins each of 3150 Dusty Rose Very Lt. (818) and 6258 Willow Green (987). Buy one skein of each remaining color.

Making the first cross-stitch: With cloth held vertically, measure across 3½″ from bottom left corner; measure downwards 25″ from top left corner. Mark point where two measurements intersect (Illus. 52). Refer to chart. Start sewing at arrow.

Finishing directions

1. Sew entire design at bottom of runner. When done, turn cloth upside down. From left tip of light green leaf, measure 12½″ downwards. Mark cloth with pin. Extend five red vertical lines down to pin. Also at pin, start sewing tip of light green leaf and rest of design for second time (Illus. 53 and 54). Finally, connect five red vertical lines to link top and bottom of runner.

2. Before edges of runner are finished off, two margins need to be added. First, on all four sides of cloth, count out

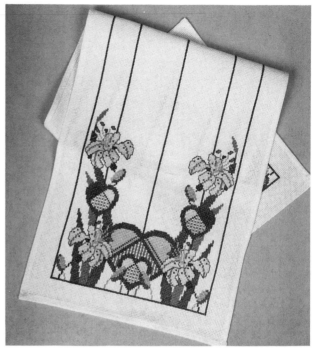

Runner

margins of seventeen squares from red border. Mark cloth with pins. Then using knotted single strand of thread, connect and hand-stitch these lines by following one row in Aida and by weaving in and out cloth with ½″ running stitches (Illus. 55). These stitches now form new edges of needlework.

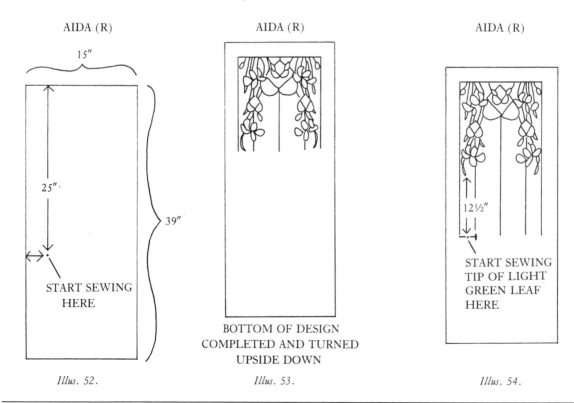

AIDA (R)

15″

25″

39″

START SEWING HERE

Illus. 52.

AIDA (R)

BOTTOM OF DESIGN COMPLETED AND TURNED UPSIDE DOWN

Illus. 53.

AIDA (R)

12½″

START SEWING TIP OF LIGHT GREEN LEAF HERE

Illus. 54.

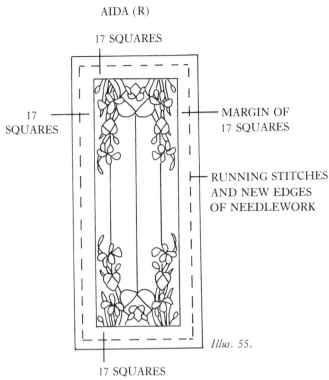

AIDA (R)

17 SQUARES

17 SQUARES

— MARGIN OF
17 SQUARES

— RUNNING STITCHES
AND NEW EDGES
OF NEEDLEWORK

Illus. 55.

17 SQUARES

4. Finish off edges of runner. To do, press back seam allowances on sides of runner. Then turn under ¼″ on raw edges, folding towards running stitches. Press. Pin. Repeat same procedure on top and bottom edges (Illus. 57).

5. On back of project, machine-stitch close to folded inner edges, pivoting at corners (Illus. 58). Use white thread.

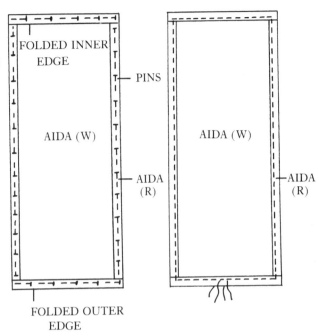

FOLDED INNER
EDGE

— PINS

AIDA (W)

AIDA (W)

— AIDA
(R)

— AIDA
(R)

FOLDED OUTER
EDGE

Illus. 57.   *Illus. 58.*

3. Add second margin to runner. On all four sides of Aida, count out from running stitches a seam allowance of seven squares. Mark cloth with pins. Cut off excess Aida at pins (Illus. 56).

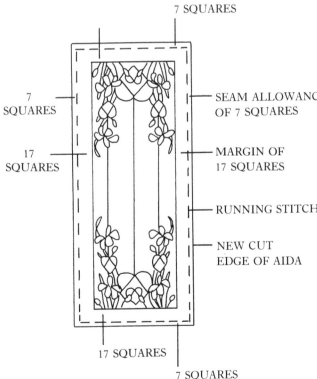

AIDA (R)

7 SQUARES

7
SQUARES

17
SQUARES

— SEAM ALLOWANCE
OF 7 SQUARES

— MARGIN OF
17 SQUARES

— RUNNING STITCHES

— NEW CUT
EDGE OF AIDA

17 SQUARES

7 SQUARES

Illus. 56.

CROSS-STITCH KEY (use two strands)

Symbol	J. & P. Coats	DMC
·	3150 Dusty Rose Very Lt.	818
⊠	3046 Christmas Red Bright	666
T	2099 Pumpkin	971
S	5471 Coffee Brown	433
■	6020 Nile Green	954
U	3128 Carnation Dk.	602
O	6256 Parrot Green Med.	581
=	6258 Willow Green	987
◆	7159 Blue Very Lt.	827
╱	3000 Garnet	816
☐	Cloth as is	

BACKSTITCH KEY (use two strands)

Symbol	J. & P. Coats	DMC
	3046 Christmas Red Bright	666

Backstitch Area: 3046 Christmas Red Bright (or 666)—Everything.

Chart on following page.

GIFTS FOR FAMILY AND FRIENDS

Fruit and Ivy *(In color on page M.)* *(Simple.)*

Size: Embroidery approximately 4″ wide × 2⅝″.

Aida 14, ivory: Premade pot holder by Charles Craft. Pot holder 8″ wide × 8½″.

Embroidery floss: Coats 5000 Russet (or DMC 435), 5472 Coffee Brown Med. (801), 5942 Tan Brown Lt. (437), 6239 Parrot Green Dk. (702), 6001 Parrot Green Lt. (907), 2307 Christmas Gold (783), 2290 Canary Bright (307), 4101 Violet Dk. (552), 4104 Lavender Dk. (554), use DMC color (3607), 3021 Christmas Red Dk. (815), 2330 Burnt Orange (947), and use DMC color (890). Purchase one skein of each.

Making the first cross-stitch: See Steps 1 and 2.

Finishing directions

1. With pot holder turned upside down, measure across 2⅞″ from left finished edge. From inner edge of bias tape, count up 41 squares on Aida. Mark point where two measurements intersect (Illus. 59). Refer to chart. Start sewing at arrow. Check also to see that there are two blank spaces between bottom of design and inner edge bias tape.

2. Pot holder and chart are intentionally turned upside down to make embroidering easier.

Pot holder

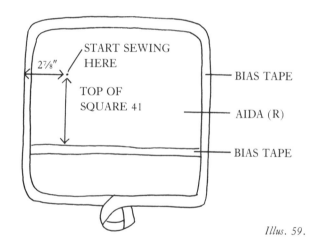

Illus. 59.

CROSS-STITCH KEY (use two strands)

Symbol	J. & P. Coats	DMC
=	5000 Russet	435
■	5472 Coffee Brown Med.	801
·	5942 Tan Brown Lt.	437
○	6239 Parrot Green Dk.	702
L	6001 Parrot Green Lt.	907
e	2307 Christmas Gold	783
z	2290 Canary Bright	307
◆	4101 Violet Dk.	552
з	4104 Lavender Dk.	554
T	Use DMC color	3607
╱	3021 Christmas Red Dk.	815
V	2330 Burnt Orange	947
⊠	Use DMC color	890
□	Cloth as is	

BACKSTITCH KEY (use two strands)

Symbol	J. & P. Coats	DMC
	5472 Coffee Brown Med.	801
	2307 Christmas Gold	783
	6001 Parrot Green Lt.	907

Backstitch Area: 5472 Coffee Brown Med. (or 801)—Stems on grapes, leaves, and pear, and outline around rim and bottom of basket. 2307 Christmas Gold (783)—Outline around banana and grapefruit. 6001 Parrot Green Lt. (907)—Veins within dark leaves.

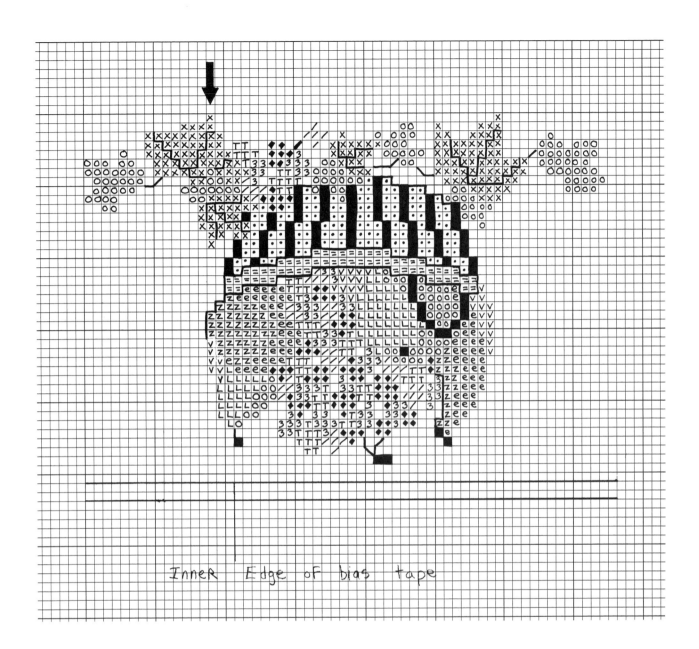

Inner Edge of bias tape

Three Bushels in Repeat *(In color on page G.) (Simple.)*

Size: Band approximately 24¼″ wide × 1″.

Maxi-weave Ribband, 14-count, white with red edging, 1″ wide: Cut band 31½″.

Embroidery floss: Coats 5000 Russet (or DMC 435), 3046 Christmas Red Bright (666), 6211 Jade Very Dk. (561), 2307 Christmas Gold (783), and 8403 Black (310). Purchase one skein of each.

Other Materials: Red basket, 8″ wide × 4″ high × 4″ deep, top rim 24¼″ around (Illus. 60). Green satin ribbon, double-faced, ⅛″ wide × 3 yards. Wire, two pieces, each 9″.

Basket band

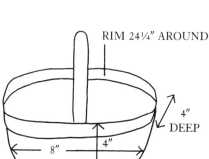
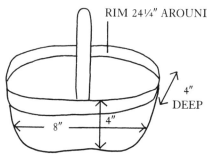

RIM 24¼″ AROUND

4″ DEEP

8″   4″

Illus. 60.

Making the first cross-stitch: Measure across 3″ from left end of horizontally held Ribband. See Step 1.

Finishing directions

1. Before doing embroidery, check measurement around top rim of your basket. If yours is not 24¼″, add or subtract embroidery. If alterations are necessary, keep sewing and trying Ribband on rim to make sure start and finish carry a complete bushel. Do not overlap embroidery. Refer to chart. Start sewing at arrow.

2. Attach Ribband to rim. Center two big green bushels in middle of front. At start of embroidery, leave 1″ of plain Ribband. Mark cloth with pin. Press back cloth at pin.

Leave ½″ of Ribband; cut off excess fabric. At end, overlap beginning of band. Press back cloth. Leave ½″ of Ribband; cut off excess. Slip-stitch or glue ends together (Illus. 61).

3. Make two bows. Cut ribbon into four pieces: Two measuring 1¼ yards each and two measuring 9″ each. Single knot ends of each ribbon. From each 1¼-yard piece, make one bow about 4½″ wide by looping ribbon back and forth. Tie center of each bow with one 9″ ribbon; knot twice on back.

4. On back of each bow, slip one wire under and through center knot (Illus. 62). Attach one bow to each side basket handle by twisting ends together.

BACK OF BASKET

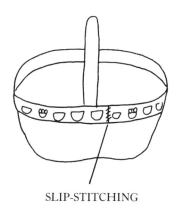

SLIP-STITCHING

Illus. 61.

BACK OF BOW

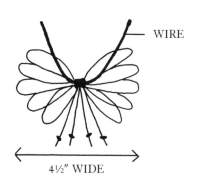

WIRE

4½″ WIDE

Illus. 62.

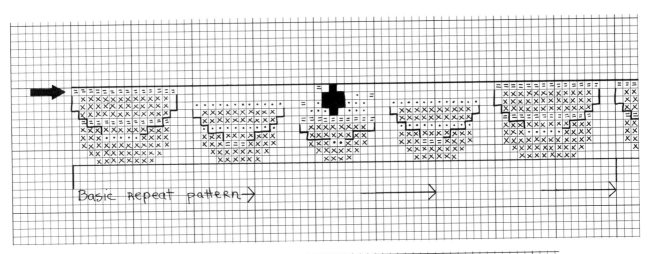

Basic repeat pattern→

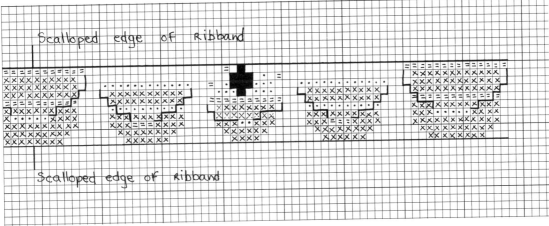

Scalloped edge of ribband

Scalloped edge of ribband

CROSS-STITCH KEY (use two strands)

Symbol	J. & P. Coats	DMC
⊠	5000 Russet	435
·	3046 Christmas Red Bright	666
≡	6211 Jade Very Dk.	561
■	2307 Christmas Gold	783
☐	Cloth as is	

BACKSTITCH KEY (use two strands)

Symbol	J. & P. Coats	DMC
	8403 Black	310

Backstitch Area: 8403 Black (or 310)—Everything.

Horse and Rider *(In color on page P.) (Simple.)*

Size: Embroidered rectangle approximately 9½″ wide × 5¾″.

Aida 14, ivory: Cut cloth 12″ wide × 8½″.

Embroidery floss: Coats 7159 Blue Very Lt. (or DMC 827), 5942 Tan Brown Lt. (437), 5360 Beige Brown Very Dk. (838), 7022 Cornflower Blue Dk. (792), 2307 Christmas Gold (783), 2293 Yellow Dark (743), use DMC color (918), 5000 Russet (435), 8403 Black (310), and 8401 Steel Grey (318). Purchase two skeins of 5000 Russet (435). Buy one skein of each remaining color.

Other materials: Basswood Country Plank by Walnut Hollow Farm (unfinished wood, outer dimensions of 11″ wide × 8″ including bark, style #3500). Muslin, for backing, 12″ wide × 8½″. Stitch Witchery, 12″ wide × 8½″. Dark brown suede or nylon cording, ⅛″ wide × 1 yard. Sawtooth picture hanger. White glue.

Making the first cross-stitch: Measure across 2⅜″ from top left corner; measure downwards 1¾″ from top left corner. Mark point where two measurements intersect. Refer to chart. Start sewing at arrow.

Finishing directions

1. Bond Aida to muslin with Stitch Witchery. With right sides up, place muslin flat, add Stitch Witchery, and position embroidery on top. Line up edges. Follow Stitch Witchery directions for bonding. Test for adhesion. Let fabric cool.
2. On each side of design, locate outer edges of embroidery. From these points, count out margins of six squares each. Mark cloth with pins. With knotted single strand of beige thread, connect and hand-stitch these lines by following one row in Aida/Stitch Witchery/muslin and by weaving in and out cloth with ½″ running stitches. These stitches now form new edges of needlework (Illus. 63).
3. Apply glue to back edges of Aida combination and in center under horse. Center Aida combination on plank. Let dry.

Wall plaque

4. With right sides up, glue suede over edges of Aida combination. Start in middle of bottom. Butt ends together. As glue hardens keep pressing suede in place. Let dry.
5. Center sawtooth picture hanger along top black edge of plank.

CROSS-STITCH KEY (use two strands)

Symbol	J. & P. Coats	DMC
⊠	7159 Blue Very Lt.	827
◆	5942 Tan Brown Lt.	437
▣	5360 Beige Brown Very Dk.	838
Ⓢ	7022 Cornflower Blue Dk.	792
ⓔ	2307 Christmas Gold	783
△	2293 Yellow Dark	743
▭	Use DMC color	918
·	5000 Russet	435
■	8403 Black	310
♥	8401 Steel Grey	318
▢	Cloth as is	

BACKSTITCH KEY (use two strands)

Symbol	J. & P. Coats	DMC
	7022 Cornflower Blue Dk.	792
	8403 Black	310

Backstitch Area: 7022 Cornflower Blue Dk. (or 792)—Lines within lettering. 8403 Black (310)—Outlines around and within horse and rider.

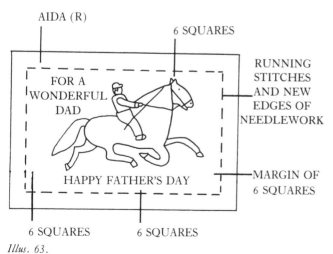

AIDA (R)

6 SQUARES

FOR A WONDERFUL DAD

HAPPY FATHER'S DAY

RUNNING STITCHES AND NEW EDGES OF NEEDLEWORK

MARGIN OF 6 SQUARES

6 SQUARES   6 SQUARES

Illus. 63.

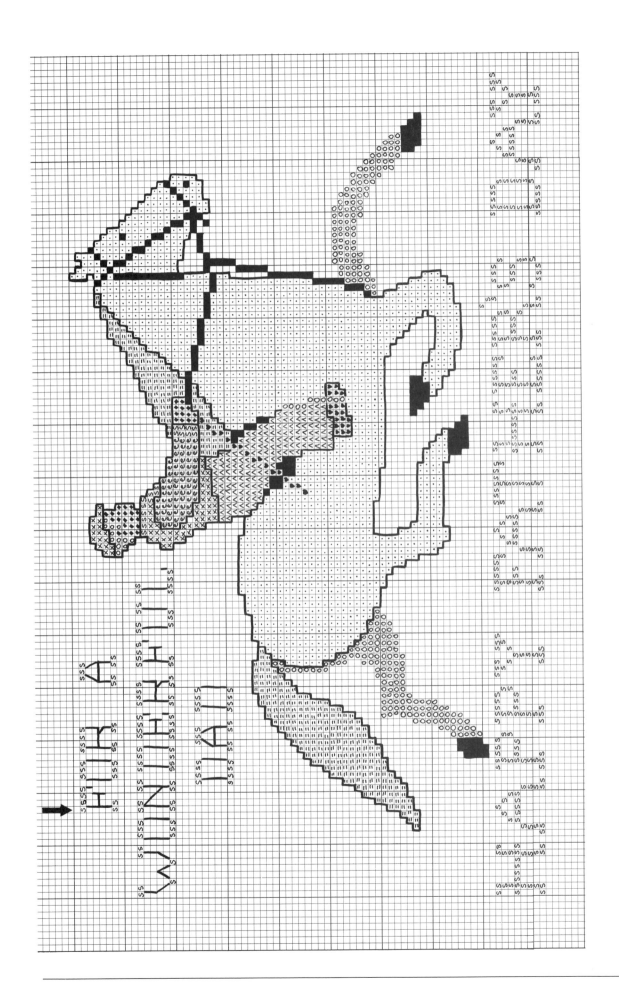

Chickens *(In color on page N.)* *(Intermediate.)*

Size: Four squares of birds and one geometric motif, each approximately 2″ square.

Trevira®/Viscose, 14-count, ivory: Premade breadcover by Charles Craft. 18″ square including fringe.

Embroidery floss: Coats 3046 Christmas Red Bright (or DMC 666), 8403 Black (310), 5470 no name (433), 3021 Christmas Red Dk. (498), and 2307 Christmas Gold (783). Purchase two skeins each of 3046 Christmas Red Bright (666) and 5470 no name (433). Buy one skein of each remaining color.

Making the first cross-stitch: See Steps 1–6.

Finishing directions

1. This design is composed of three elements: A striped border which is interrupted at each corner with a single gold diamond; four birds (designs one and two) positioned in the corners; and a geometric motif (design three) in the center of the fabric. Position these elements as shown. Designs one, two, and border are stitched on right side of cloth. Design three is worked on wrong side (Illus. 64).

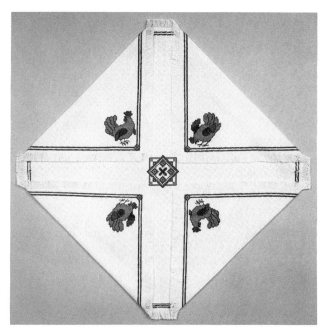

Bread cover

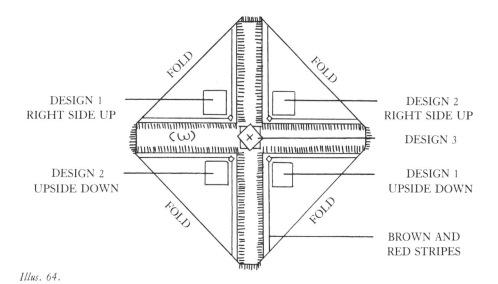

Illus. 64.

2. To begin, sew continuous brown and red border. On all four sides of cloth, count in margin of three squares from fringe. Cross-stitch brown stripe. Leave margin of one square. Cross-stitch red stripe. Refer to designs one and two for placement of single diamond in each corner.

3. Prepare cloth for designs one and two. Each bird is 26 stitches wide and 28 stitches high. To make sewing easier, block out areas to be embroidered. Mark cloth with pins. Then using knotted single strand of thread, connect and hand-stitch these lines by following one row in fabric and by weaving in and out cloth with ½″ running stitches. Refer to charts. Start sewing at arrows.

4. Turn cloth upside down. Embroider designs one and two for second time.

5. Prepare cloth for design three. Locate center of bread-cloth by folding fabric in quarters. Mark center with pin (Illus. 65).

6. Open cloth as shown (Illus. 66). At pin, make one black cross-stitch which corresponds to center of design three. Refer to chart. Count up squares to top of geometric motif. Mark cloth with pin. Start sewing at arrow.

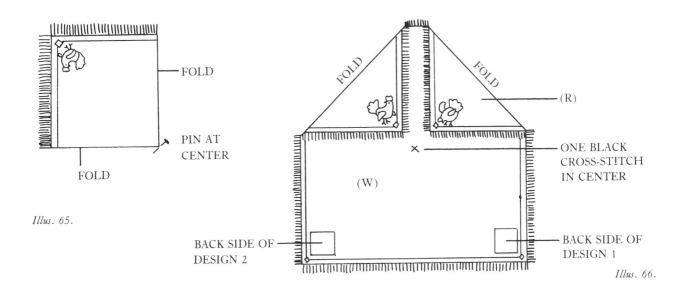

FOLD

PIN AT CENTER

FOLD

Illus. 65.

FOLD

FOLD

(R)

ONE BLACK CROSS-STITCH IN CENTER

(W)

BACK SIDE OF DESIGN 2

BACK SIDE OF DESIGN 1

Illus. 66.

CROSS-STITCH KEY (use two strands)

Symbol	J. & P. Coats	DMC
◆	3046 *Christmas Red Bright*	666
⊠	8403 *Black*	310
▣	5470 *no name*	433
▣	3021 *Christmas Red Dk.*	498
▣	2307 *Christmas Gold*	783
▢	*Cloth as is*	

BACKSTITCH KEY (use two strands)

Symbol	J. & P. Coats	DMC
	8403 *Black*	310

Backstitch Area: 8403 Black (or 310)—Everything.

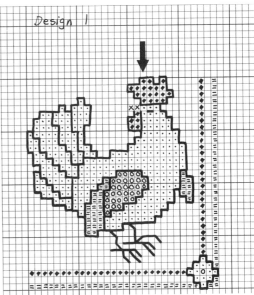

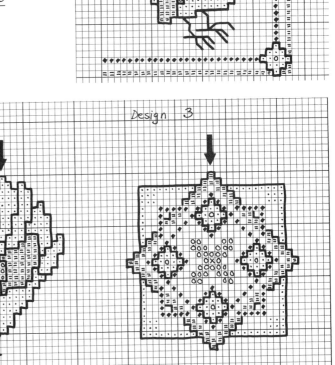

Tropical Fish *(In color on page A.) (Intermediate.)*

Size: Embroidery approximately 7¾" wide × 11".

Aida 8, white: Cut cloth 13½" wide × 17".

Embroidery floss: Coats 2290 Canary Bright (or DMC 973), 8403 Black (310), 7001 Peacock Blue (use Coats color), 2330 Burnt Orange (947), 3046 Christmas Red Bright (666), 4101 Violet Dk. (552), 7159 Blue Very Lt. (827), 6239 Parrot Green Dk. (702), and 7023 Blue Med. (797). Purchase two skeins each of 8403 Black (310) and 7159 Blue Very Lt. (827). Buy one skein of each remaining color.

Other materials: Rectangular red plastic tote bag with small grid pattern, 15" wide at base (16" wide at top edge) × 12¾" high × 5½" deep (Illus. 67). White cotton, for backing, 13½" wide × 17". Red maxi piping, 1¼ yards.

Tote bag

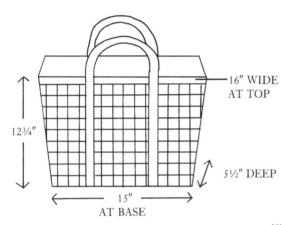

Illus. 67.

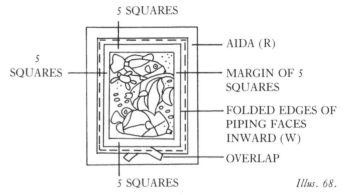

Illus. 68.

Making the first cross-stitch: Measure across 3½" from top left corner; measure downwards 3½" from top left corner. Mark point where two measurements intersect. Refer to chart. Start sewing at arrow.

Finishing directions

1. From all four sides of design, add margin of five squares. Mark cloth with pins. Using knotted single strand of white thread, connect and hand-stitch these lines by following one row in Aida and by weaving in and out cloth with ½" running stitches. These stitches now form new edges of needlework.

2. Baste piping to right side of Aida. Begin in middle of bottom. Position folded edges of piping towards center of design. Turn ends downward at start and finish. Arrange so that commercial stitching line on piping rests on white running stitches. Overlap ends by 1" (Illus. 68).

3. Machine-stitch piping to Aida. Sew on commercial stitching line in piping, pivoting at corners (Illus. 69). Use white thread.

4. With right sides together, pin Aida on backing with piping wedged in between. Machine-stitch, using seam lines in Step 3 as your guide, pivoting at corners. Leave 3" opening in middle of one side. Trim seams to ⅝". Slash corners on diagonal (Illus. 70).

5. Turn. Press. Slip-stitch opening closed.

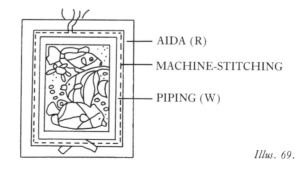

Illus. 69.

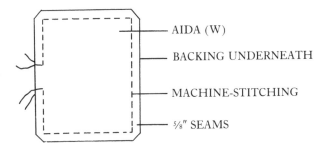

- AIDA (W)
- BACKING UNDERNEATH
- MACHINE-STITCHING
- ⅝" SEAMS

Illus. 70.

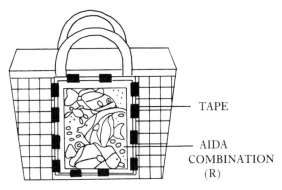

- TAPE
- AIDA COMBINATION (R)

Illus. 71.

6. With rights sides up, center Aida combination on tote. Attach temporarily with masking tape (Illus. 71). Then using double strand red thread, tack Aida to grid. To do, take one small running stitch on back of piping. Go down and behind one grid. Come up taking another small running stitch in piping. Repeat. Or, if you prefer, apply glue along back of piping. Position embroidered rectangle on plastic. Let dry.

CROSS-STITCH KEY (use three strands)

Symbol	J. & P. Coats	DMC
e	2290 Canary Bright	973
⊠	8403 Black	310
⊡	7001 Peacock Blue	Use J. & P. Coats color
⊟	2330 Burnt Orange	947
T	3046 Christmas Red Bright	666
U	4101 Violet Dk.	552
·	7159 Blue Very Lt.	827
◆	6239 Parrot Green Dk.	702
▲	7023 Blue Med.	797
☐	Cloth as is	

BACKSTITCH KEY (use two strands)

Symbol	J. & P. Coats	DMC
	8403 Black	310

Backstitch Area: 8403 Black (or 310)—Everything.

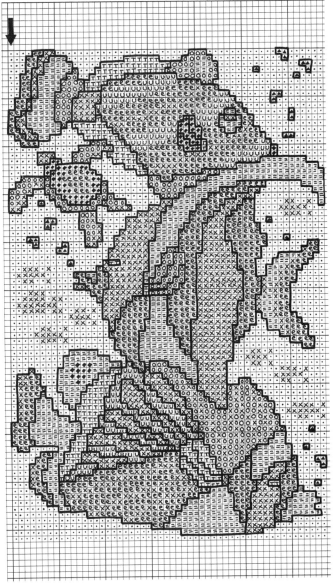

Geometric Heart Set *(In color on page H.)* *(Intermediate.)*

Coordinated towels

Size: Embroidery on each towel approximately 6⅝″ wide × 2½″.

Aida 14, white: Three premade towels by Charles Craft. Each fringed towel is 14½″ wide × 24½″ (kitchen mates style TT-6100).

Embroidery floss: Coats 7021 Delft (or DMC 809), 3153 Geranium (956), 3281 Pink Med. (963), 3021 Christmas Red Dk. (815), 5363 Old Gold Lt. (use Coats color), and 7100 Royal Blue Dk. (796). Purchase three skeins of 7021 Delft (809). Buy one skein of each remaining color for set.

Making the first cross-stitch: See Step 1.

Finishing directions

1. Since your Aida borders may differ in size from mine, count horizontal and vertical squares on yours. Each design is 89 stitches wide and 35 stitches high. Subtract required figures from yours. Divide unused figures by two. Arrange these numbers as margins on either side of design (mine were fifty squares on sides and three squares at top and bottom). Mark cloth with pins. Block out area to be embroidered. Using knotted single strand of thread, connect and hand-stitch these lines by following one row in Aida and by weaving in and out cloth with ½″ running stitches (Illus. 72). Refer to charts. Start sewing at arrows.

2. Fold each towel in thirds with embroidery centered on top.

Illus. 72.

TOWEL (R)

14-COUNT BORDER

3 SQUARES

AREA TO BE EMBROIDERED

50 SQUARES

MARGIN OF 50 SQUARES

3 SQUARES

RUNNING STITCHES

CROSS-STITCH KEY (use two strands)

Symbol	J. & P. Coats	DMC
⊠	7021 Delft	809
·	3153 Geranium	956
⊟	3281 Pink Med.	963
■	3021 Christmas Red Dk.	815
◆	5363 Old Gold Lt.	Use J. & P. Coats color
⊡	7100 Royal Blue Dk.	796
☐	Cloth as is	

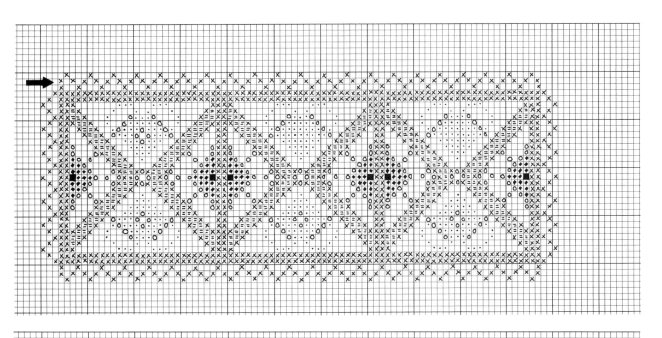

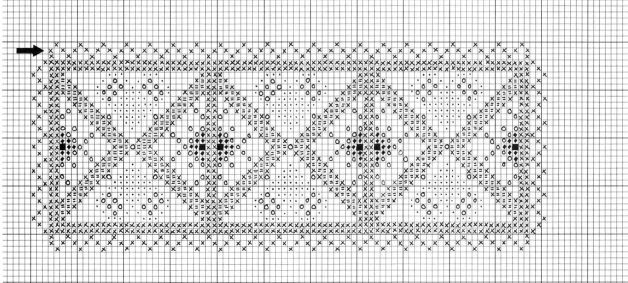

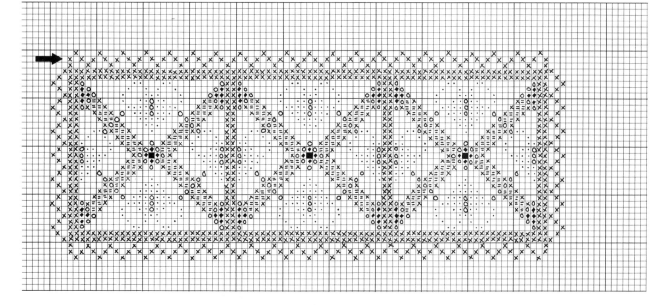

Daffodils *(In color on page E.)* *(Intermediate.)*

Size: Embroidery approximately 8″ in diameter.

Aida 11, ivory: Cut cloth 15″ square.

Embroidery floss: Coats 2294 Topaz Lt. (or DMC 726), 6020 Nile Green Lt. (954), 2292 Golden Yellow Very Lt. (3078), 2099 Pumpkin (971), 2303 Tangerine Lt. (742), 5472 Coffee Brown Med. (801), 5365 no name (435), 6256 Parrot Green Med. (704), 6211 Jade Very Dk. (561), and 6226 Kelly Green (701). Purchase two skeins of 6226 Kelly Green (701). Buy one skein of each remaining color.

Other materials: Sudberry House Crown Plate (11½″ in diameter, woodstain with 8″ round design area, style #18081). 100% polyester batting, 10″ square. Eight small wire nails, ½ × 19 flat head. One sawtooth picture hanger. Masking tape. Tracing paper. White glue.

Making the first cross-stitch: Measure across 7″ from top left corner; measure downwards 3¼″ from top left corner. Mark point where two measurements intersect. Refer to chart. Start sewing at arrow.

Finishing directions

1. Press out mounting board and two backing papers from crown plate.
2. With right sides up, place mounting board in center of tracing paper. With pencil trace around cardboard. Remove cardboard. From edges of outline, add 1½″ margins. At frequent intervals, mark paper with dots. Connect dots to form larger circle (Illus. 73).
3. Fold tracing paper circle in half and then in quarters (Illus. 74). This pattern will be used to cut out Aida.
4. With right sides up, center inner circle and fold lines in tracing paper over embroidery. Place crown plate on top to check that design looks centered, lettering is well positioned, and ends of leaves are covered by frame. Make any adjustments. Pin. Cut out Aida on new edge of circle line.
5. Cut polyester batting same size as mounting board. With right sides up, tape batting to mounting board in north-south-east-west position.

Birthday plate

6. To prevent Aida from unravelling, machine-stitch ¼″ from edge of circle.
7. With 36″ strand of floss, make ½″ running stitches ¼″ to inside of machine-stitching. Start and finish at top. Even up ends of floss (Illus. 75).
8. With right sides down, center batting/mounting board over Aida. Gather up circle by pulling in on floss. Put Aida combination in plate to check design. Make any adjustments. Knot.
9. Top back of plate with backing paper one. To permanently hold everything in position, hammer nails into edges of circle (Illus. 76).
10. Glue and center backing paper two over back edges of plate.
11. Center sawtooth picture hanger along top back edge of plate.

TRACING PAPER

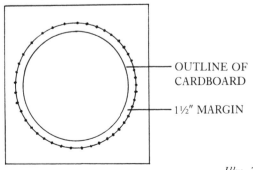

—— OUTLINE OF CARDBOARD

—— 1½″ MARGIN

Illus. 73.

TRACING PAPER

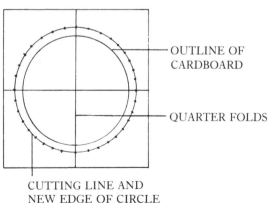

—— OUTLINE OF CARDBOARD

—— QUARTER FOLDS

CUTTING LINE AND NEW EDGE OF CIRCLE

Illus. 74.

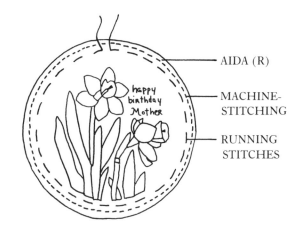

Illus. 75.

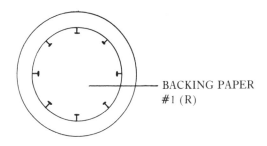

BACKING PAPER
#1 (R)

Illus. 76.

CROSS-STITCH KEY (use two strands)

Symbol	J. & P. Coats	DMC
⊡	2294 Topaz Lt.	726
⊡	6020 Nile Green Lt.	954
T	2292 Golden Yellow Very Lt.	3078
■	2099 Pumpkin	971
╱	2303 Tangerine Lt.	742
▲	5472 Coffee Brown Med.	801
S	5365 no name	435
⊠	6256 Parrot Green Med.	704
e	6211 Jade Very Dk.	561
=	6226 Kelly Green	701
☐	Cloth as is	

BACKSTITCH KEY (use two strands)

Symbol	J. & P. Coats	DMC
	6211 Jade Very Dk.	561

Backstitch Area: 6211 Jade Very Dk. (or 561)—Everything.

Chart on following page.

happy
birthday
Mother

Folk Art Set *(In color on page M.) (Intermediate.)*

Size: Embroidery on each pot holder approximately 4⅞" wide × 4⅜". Embroidery on towel approximately 6⅜" wide × 2⅞".

Aida 14, ecru: Premade pot holders and towel by Charles Craft. Each pot holder is 8" wide × 7⅝" with 14-count border measuring 7" wide × 5⅝" (kitchen mates style PH-6201). Towel is 16½" wide × 27" with 14-count border measuring 16½" wide × 2⅞".

Embroidery floss: Coats 6211 Jade Very Dk. (or DMC 991), 2326 Copper (921), 5471 Coffee Brown (801), and 5363 Old Gold Lt. (use Coats color). Purchase three skeins each of 2326 Copper (921) and 5363 Old Gold Lt. (use Coats color). Purchase two skeins of 5471 Coffee Brown (801). Buy one skein of each remaining color for set.

Making the first cross-stitch: See Steps 1 and 2.

Finishing directions

1. Since your pot holders may differ in size from mine, count horizontal and vertical squares on yours. Turn pot holders upside down to make embroidering easier. Count from edges of bias tape. "Bull" and "Rooster" are each 68 stitches wide and 59 stitches high. Subtract required figures from yours. Divide unused figures by two for sides and by three for tops and bottoms. Arrange these numbers as margins on either side of design (mine were fourteen on sides of "Bull," fifteen on sides of "Rooster," and six and thirteen squares on tops and bottoms of both). Mark cloth with pins. Block out areas to be embroidered. Using knotted single strand of thread, connect and hand-stitch these lines by following one row in Aida and by weaving in and out cloth with ½" running stitches (Illus. 77). Refer to charts. Start sewing at arrows.

Coordinated pot holders and towel

2. Turn pot holders upside down. Pot holders and charts are intentionally turned upside down to make embroidering easier.

3. Since your towel border may differ from mine, count horizontal and vertical squares on yours. "Horse" is 91 stitches wide and 40 stitches high. Subtract required figures from yours. Divide unused figures by two. Arrange these numbers as margins on either side of design (mine were seventy squares on sides and zero squares on top and bottom). Mark cloth with pins. Block out area to be embroidered as in Step 1 (Illus. 78). Refer to chart. Start sewing at arrow.

4. Fold towel in thirds with embroidery centered on top.

Chart and Cross-Stitch Key on following pages.

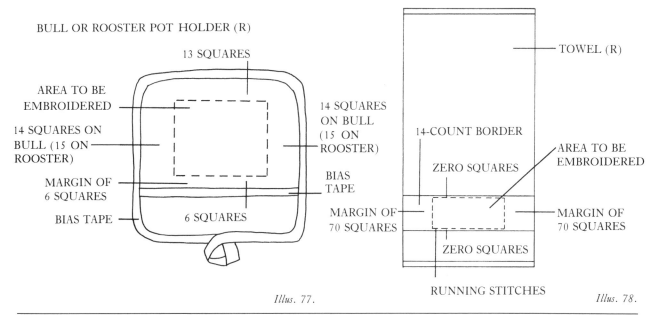

BULL OR ROOSTER POT HOLDER (R)

13 SQUARES

AREA TO BE EMBROIDERED

14 SQUARES ON BULL (15 ON ROOSTER)

MARGIN OF 6 SQUARES

BIAS TAPE

6 SQUARES

14 SQUARES ON BULL (15 ON ROOSTER)

BIAS TAPE

Illus. 77.

TOWEL (R)

14-COUNT BORDER

ZERO SQUARES

AREA TO BE EMBROIDERED

MARGIN OF 70 SQUARES

ZERO SQUARES

MARGIN OF 70 SQUARES

RUNNING STITCHES

Illus. 78.

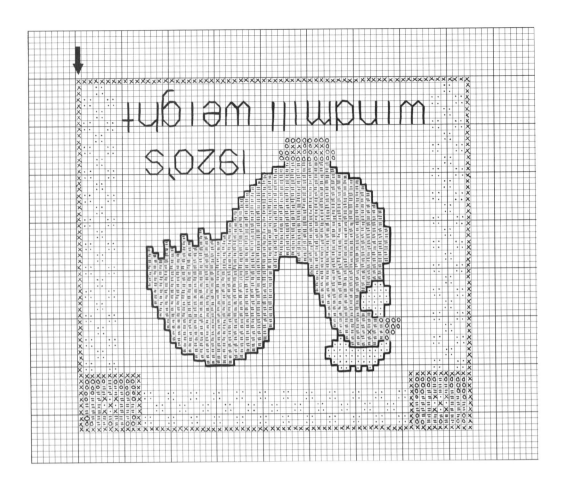

windmill weight
1920's

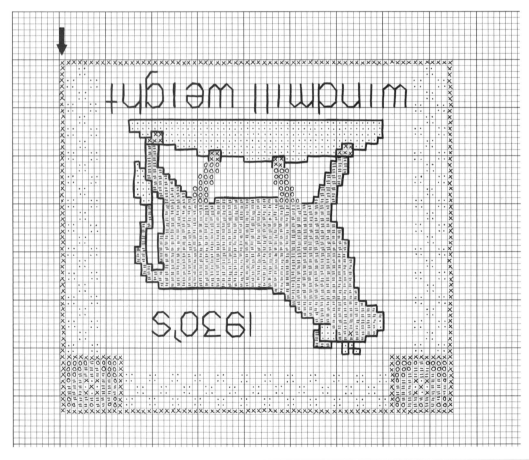

windmill weight
1930's

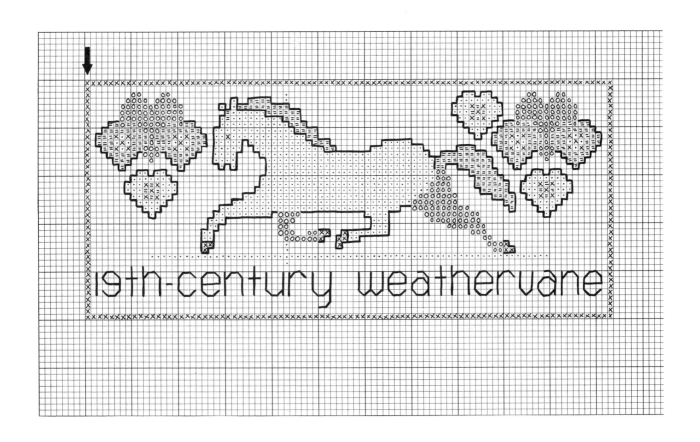

CROSS-STITCH KEY (use two strands)

Symbol	J. & P. Coats	DMC
⊠	6211 Jade Very Dk.	991
·	2326 Copper	921
⊡	5471 Coffee Brown	801
⊟	5363 Old Gold Lt.	Use J. & P. Coats color
☐	Cloth as is	

BACKSTITCH KEY (use two strands)

Symbol	J. & P. Coats	DMC
	5471 Coffee Brown	801

Backstitch Area: 5471 Coffee Brown (or 801)—Everything.

Cyclamen *(In color on page G.)* *(Advanced.)*

Size: Embroidery approximately 10½″ square.

Aida 8, white: Cut cloth 16″ square.

Embroidery floss: Coats 6239 Parrot Green Dk. (or DMC 702), 6030 Nile Green Lt. (954), use DMC color (369), 6228 Christmas Green (909), 6001 Parrot Green Lt. (907), 6267 Avocado Green (469), 3021 Christmas Red Dk. (815), 3056 Watermelon (600), 3063 Cranberry (602), 3281 Pink Med. (776), 2290 Canary Bright (973), use DMC color (610), 5363 Old Gold Lt. (783), 5470 no name (433), 5371 Topaz Very Ultra Dk. (435), and 5472 Coffee Brown Med. (801). Purchase two skeins of 6228 Christmas Green (909). Buy one skein of each remaining color.

Other materials: White cotton, for back and ruffle, ¾ yard. Pink maxi piping, 1½ yards. Tracing paper. 12″ square pillow insert.

Making the first cross-stitch: Measure across 6″ from top left corner; measure downwards 2⅝″ from top left corner. Mark point where two measurements intersect. Refer to chart. Start sewing at arrow.

Finishing directions

1. Make pillow patterns for front (Illus. 79) and back (Illus. 80).

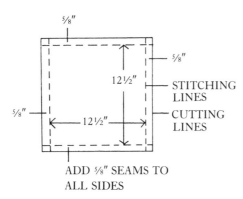

Illus. 79.

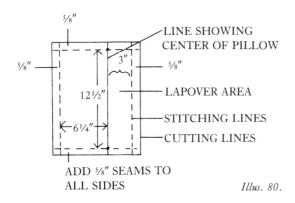

Illus. 80.

Pillow

2. With right sides up, lay front pattern over Aida. Center design (margins should be about 1″ on all sides). Pin. Cut. Transfer stitching lines to wrong side front.

3. Lay out and cut back. Transfer stitching lines and dots to wrong side cloth.

4. With right sides together, baste piping on front. Begin in middle of bottom. Position folded edge of piping towards center of design. Turn ends downwards at start and finish. Arrange so that commercial stitching line on piping rests on stitching line transferred to wrong side front. Overlap ends by 1″ (Illus. 81).

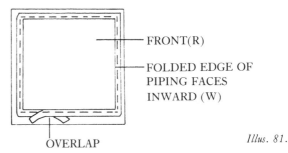

Illus. 81.

5. For ruffle, cut three strips of fabric each 4″ wide and 40″ long.

6. With right sides together, stitch together three ruffle sections. Make ½″ seams. Press open.

7. Narrow-hem bottom of ruffle. To do, turn up ½″ seam allowance on lower edge. Press. Turn under ¼″ on raw edge. Press. Pin. Machine-stitch close to inner edge (Illus. 82).

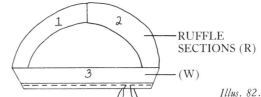

Illus. 82.

8. Prepare top of ruffle for gathering. First, divide ruffle in half by starting at one seam and marking midway point on opposite side. With sewing machine set for long basting stitches, stitch ½″ from upper edges, breaking at midpoints. Stitch again ¼″ away in seam allowances (Illus. 83).

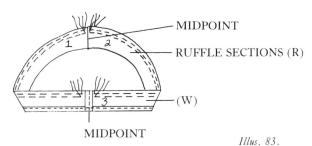

MIDPOINT

RUFFLE SECTIONS (R)

(W)

MIDPOINT

Illus. 83.

9. With right sides together, put half of ruffle on front. Start by placing one seam in upper left corner and halfway point in lower right corner. Get ½″ stitching lines on ruffle to rest on stitching lines transferred to wrong side front. Adjust gathers. Pin (Illus. 84). Piping is wedged in between ruffle and front.

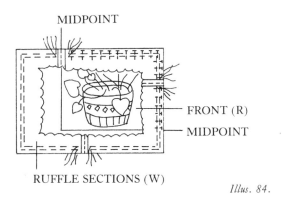

MIDPOINT

FRONT (R)

MIDPOINT

RUFFLE SECTIONS (W)

Illus. 84.

10. Gather and pin remaining half of ruffle on front.

11. Machine-stitch ruffle to front, pivoting at corners (Illus. 85). Use ½″ stitching lines on ruffle as your guide. Use white thread. Check to see that ruffle lies correctly.

12. On back sections, turn in center edge along seam line.

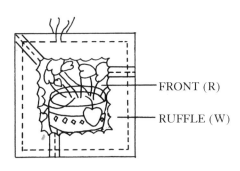

FRONT (R)

RUFFLE (W)

Illus. 85.

Press. Turn under ¼″ on raw edge. Press. Pin. Machine-stitch close to inner edge (Illus. 86).

BACK SECTIONS (W)

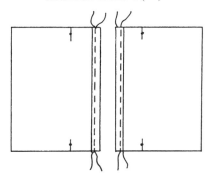

Illus. 86.

13. With right sides down, pin left back on right back matching large dots. Machine-stitch across lapover area (Illus. 87).

BACK SECTIONS (W)

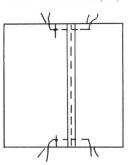

Illus. 87.

14. With right sides together, pin front on back. Machine-stitch by using seam lines in Step 11 as your guide, pivoting at corners. Trim seams to ⅝″. Slash corners on diagonal (Illus. 88).

15. Turn. Press. Push insert through slit in back of pillow.

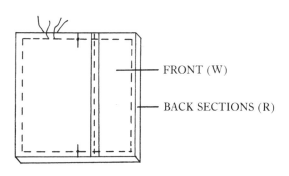

FRONT (W)

BACK SECTIONS (R)

Illus. 88.

Chart and Cross-Stitch Key on following page.

CROSS-STITCH KEY (use three strands)

Symbol	J. & P. Coats	DMC
◆	6239 Parrot Green Dk.	702
=	6030 Nile Green Lt.	954
U	Use DMC color	369
⊠	6228 Christmas Green	909
C	6001 Parrot Green Lt.	907
T	6267 Avocado Green	469
O	3021 Christmas Red Dk.	815
S	3056 Watermelon	600
△	3063 Cranberry	602
3	3281 Pink Med.	776
■	2290 Canary Bright	973
e	Use DMC color	610
·	5363 Old Gold Lt.	783

⊘	5470 no name	433
⊽	5371 Topaz Very Ultra Dk.	435
◪	5472 Coffee Brown Med.	801
☐	Cloth as is	

BACKSTITCH KEY (use two strands)

Symbol	J. & P. Coats	DMC
	3056 Watermelon	600
	3063 Cranberry	602
	5470 no name	433

Backstitch Area: 3056 Watermelon (or 600)—Outline around leaves. 3063 Cranberry (602)—Outline around flowers. 5470 no name (433)—Outline on sides of basket.

BABY GIFTS

Ducks *(In color on page F.)* *(Simple.)*

Size: Embroidery approximately 9³⁄₁₆″ wide × 2³⁄₈″.

Aida 14, yellow: Premade bib by Charles Craft. Opened bib is 10⅛″ wide × 19″ (including fringe) with 14-count border measuring 10⅛″ wide × 2⅝″.

Embroidery floss: Coats 8403 Black (or DMC 310), 7001 Peacock Blue (use Coats color), 1001 White (Snow-White), 2330 Burnt Orange (947), 5470 no name (433), 3153 Geranium (956), 7159 Blue Very Lt. (827), 6266 Apple Green (use Coats color), and 3281 Pink Med. (963). Purchase one skein of each.

Making the first cross-stitch: See Step 1.

Finishing directions

1. Since your Aida border may differ in size from mine, count horizontal and vertical squares on yours. Design is 129 stitches wide and 30 stitches high. Subtract required figures from yours. Divide unused figures by two. Arrange these numbers as margins on either side of design (mine were four squares on sides and zero squares at top and bottom). Mark cloth with pins. Block out area to be embroidered. Using knotted single strand of thread, connect and hand-stitch these lines by following one row in Aida and by weaving in and out cloth with ½″ running stitches (Illus. 89). Refer to chart. Start sewing at arrow.

Bib

Illus. 89.

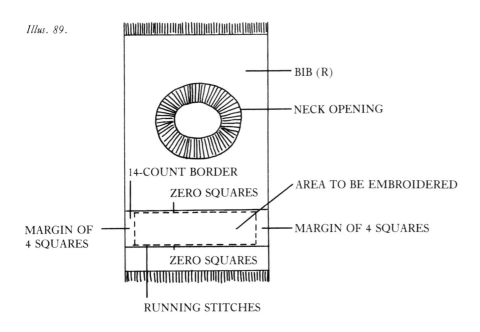

BIB (R)

NECK OPENING

14-COUNT BORDER

ZERO SQUARES

AREA TO BE EMBROIDERED

MARGIN OF 4 SQUARES

MARGIN OF 4 SQUARES

ZERO SQUARES

RUNNING STITCHES

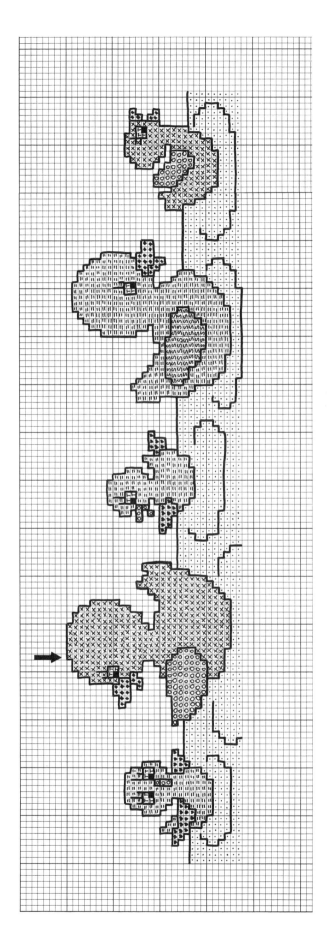

CROSS-STITCH KEY (use two strands)

Symbol	J. & P. Coats	DMC
■	8403 Black	310
⊠	7001 Peacock Blue	Use J. & P. Coats color
T	1001 White	Snow-White
◆	2330 Burnt Orange	947
⊡	5470 no name	433
⊟	3153 Geranium	956
·	7159 Blue Very Lt.	827
♥	6266 Apple Green	Use J. & P. Coats color
S	3281 Pink Med.	963
☐	Cloth as is	

BACKSTITCH KEY (use two strands)

Symbol	J. & P. Coats	DMC
	8403 Black	310

Backstitch Area: 8403 Black (or 310)—Everything.

Bears *(In color on page F.) (Simple.)*

Size: Embroidery approximately 7″ wide × 3″.

Aida 14 white: Premade bib by Janlynn Personal Wares. Edged with red bias tape, bib is 9¼″ wide × 10⅞″ with Aida inset measuring 8½″ wide × 3⅝″ (Illus. 90), style #990-5024.

BIB (R)

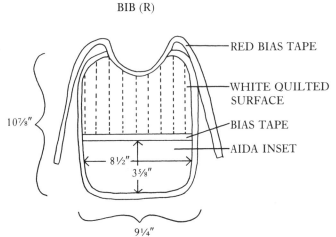

Illus. 90.

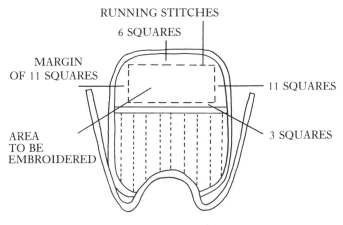

Bib

Embroidery floss: Coats 5470 no name (or DMC 433), 3046 Christmas Red Bright (666), 2293 Yellow Dark (743), 8403 Black (310), 2330 Burnt Orange (946), 7001 Peacock Blue (996), 4092 Violet Med. (552), and 6226 Kelly Green (701). Purchase two skeins of 5470 no name (433). Buy one skein of each remaining color.

Making the first cross-stitch: See Steps 1 and 2.

Finishing directions

1. Since your Aida inset may differ in size from mine, count horizontal and vertical squares across center of yours. Design is 97 stitches wide and 42 stitches high. Subtract required figures from yours. Divide unused figures for sides by two. Because of rounded corners at bottom of design, divide unused figures by three (arrange ⅓ of squares above design and ⅔ of squares below design). Arrange these numbers as margins on either side of design (mine were eleven squares on sides, three squares on top, and six squares on bottom of Aida). Mark cloth with pins. Block out area to be embroidered. Using knotted single strand of thread, connect and hand-stitch these lines by following one row in Aida and by weaving in and out cloth with ½″ running stitches (Illus. 91). Refer to chart. Start sewing at arrow.

2. Turn bib upside down. Bib and chart are intentionally turned upside down to make embroidering easier.

Illus. 91.

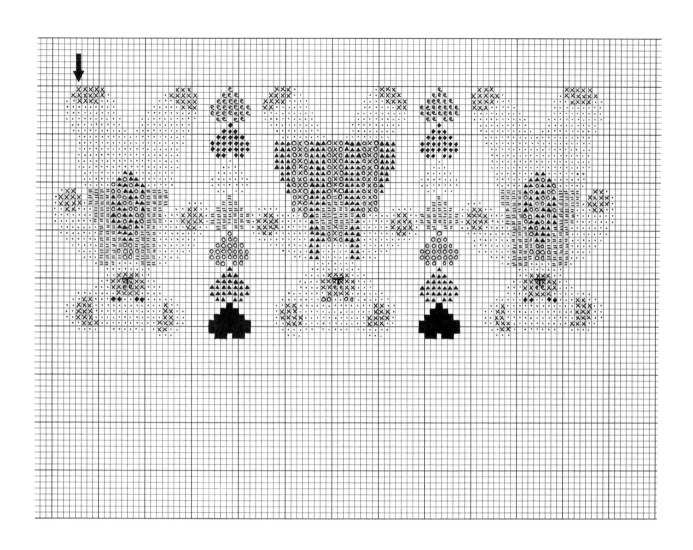

CROSS-STITCH KEY (use two strands)

Symbol	J. & P. Coats	DMC
·	5470 *no name*	*433*
=	3046 *Christmas Red Bright*	*666*
⊡	2293 *Yellow Dark*	*743*
e	8403 *Black*	*310*
⊠	2330 *Burnt Orange*	*946*
◆	7001 *Peacock Blue*	*996*
■	4092 *Violet Med.*	*552*
▲	6226 *Kelly Green*	*701*
☐	*Cloth as is*	

BACKSTITCH KEY (use two strands)

Symbol	J. & P. Coats	DMC
	8403 *Black*	*310*

Backstitch Area: 8403 Black (or 310)—Everything.

Blocks *(In color on page F.) (Simple.)*

Size: Embroidery approximately 8½″ wide × 2⅜″.

Aida 14, ivory: Premade bib by Charles Craft. Opened bib is 10¼″ wide × 18⅛″ (including fringe) with 14-count border, measuring 10¼″ wide × 2⅝″.

Embroidery floss: Coats 3046 Christmas Red Bright (or DMC 666), 7023 Blue Med. (797), 2293 Yellow Dark (743), 6256 Parrot Green Med. (use Coats color), 5470 no name (433), 3021 Christmas Red Dk. (498), use DMC color (775), 5472 Coffee Brown Med. (898), and 7021 Delft (809). Purchase one skein of each.

Making the first cross-stitch: See Step 1.

Finishing directions

1. Repeat Step 1 in "Ducks." The only exceptions are: This design is 130 stitches wide and 30 stitches high, and refer to this diagram (Illus. 92).

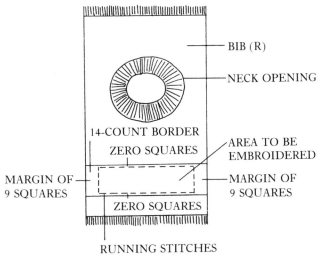

BIB (R)

NECK OPENING

14-COUNT BORDER

ZERO SQUARES

AREA TO BE EMBROIDERED

MARGIN OF 9 SQUARES

MARGIN OF 9 SQUARES

ZERO SQUARES

RUNNING STITCHES

Illus. 92.

Bib

CROSS-STITCH KEY (use two strands)

Symbol	J. & P. Coats	DMC
⊠	3046 Christmas Red Bright	666
⊙	7023 Blue Med.	797
◆	2293 Yellow Dark	743
Ⓢ	6256 Parrot Green Med.	Use J. & P. Coats color
⊟	5470 no name	433
ⓔ	3021 Christmas Red Dk.	498
·	Use DMC color	775
■	5472 Coffee Brown Med.	898
♥	7021 Delft	809
▢	Cloth as is	

BACKSTITCH KEY (use two strands)

Symbol	J. & P. Coats	DMC
	5472 Coffee Brown Med.	898
	3021 Christmas Red Dk.	498
	3046 Christmas Red Bright	666

Backstitch Area: 5472 Coffee Brown Med. (or 898)—Bear's nose, veins, and outlines around both leaves. 3021 Christmas Red Dk. (498)—Outline around top and right side of apple. 3046 Christmas Red Bright (666)—Outlines around and within bear.

Owl *(In color on page F.)* *(Simple.)*

Size: Embroidery approximately 4⅞" wide × 4⅝".

Aida 11, white: Premade bib edged with pink bias tape. Bib is 6¼" wide × 5½" (including tape) (Illus. 93).

Embroidery floss: Coats 3001 Cranberry Lt. (or DMC 604), 7030 Blue (799), 2293 Yellow Dark (743), 6256 Parrot Green Med. (use Coats color), 8403 Black (310), 2332 Burnt Orange Dk. (608), 4092 Violet Med. (552), and 5470 no name (433). Purchase one skein of each.

BIB (R)

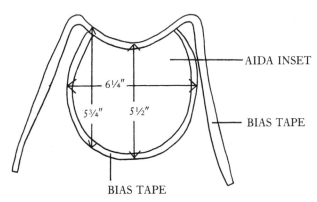

Illus. 93.

Bib

Making the first cross-stitch: See Steps 1 and 2.

Finishing directions

1. Since your bib may differ in size from mine, count horizontal and vertical squares across center of yours. "Owl" is 57 stitches wide and 53 stitches high with corners of design cut off by rounded edges of bib. Subtract required figures from yours. Divide unused figures by two. Arrange these numbers as margins (mine were three squares on sides, two squares at top, and three squares at bottom). Mark cloth with pins. Block out area to be embroidered. Using knotted single strand of thread, connect and hand-stitch these lines by following one row in Aida and by weaving in and out cloth with ½" running stitches.

2. Before sewing make sure owl's left ear, left wing, tail feathers, and yellow bird's tail fit in blocked out area (Illus. 94). If any part of design does not fit, reposition area to be embroidered. Refer to chart. Start sewing at arrow.

BIB (R)

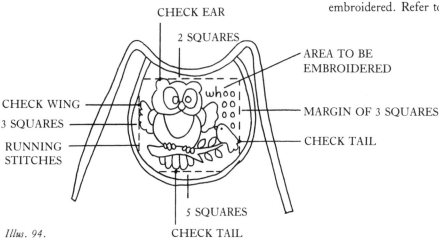

Illus. 94.

74

CROSS-STITCH KEY (use two strands)

Symbol	J. & P. Coats	DMC
⊠	3001 Cranberry Lt.	604
▣	7030 Blue	799
◈	2293 Yellow Dark	743
♥	6256 Parrot Green Med.	Use J. & P. Coats color
■	8403 Black	310
Ⓢ	2332 Burnt Orange Dk.	608
·	4092 Violet Med.	552
△	5470 no name	433
☐	Cloth as is	

BACKSTITCH KEY (use two strands)

Symbol	J. & P. Coats	DMC
	8403 Black	310

Backstitch Area: 8403 Black (or 310)—Everything.

Rabbit *(In color on page 1.)* *(Intermediate.)*

Size: Embroidery approximately 7" wide × 6¼".

Aida 14, white: Cut cloth 12" square.

Embroidery floss: Coats 7976 Baby Blue (or DMC 3325), 3067 Baby Pink (963), 5365 no name (435), 5471 Coffee Brown (433), 6267 Avocado Green (469), 2326 Copper (920), 3127 Carnation Lt. (894), and 6250 Pine Green Lt. (772). Purchase two skeins of 3067 Baby Pink (963). Buy one skein of each remaining color.

Other materials: Thin white cotton, for lining, 12" square. Rust cotton, for back, 12" square. White pregathered cotton eyelet ruffle, 1⅛" wide × 1 yard. White satin ribbon, double-faced, ⅜" wide × 15". Poly-fil 100% polyester fibre, approximately 3 ounces.

Making the first cross-stitch: Measure across 2¾" from top left corner; measure downwards 2⅝" from top left corner. Mark point where two measurements intersect. Refer to chart. Start sewing at arrow.

Finishing directions

1. With right sides up, place Aida over lining. Pin.
2. From outer edges of tallest leaves and tips of birds' tails, count out margin of six squares on all four sides of design. Mark cloth with pins. With knotted single strand of white thread, connect and hand-stitch these lines by following one row in Aida and by weaving in and out cloth with ½" running stitches (Illus. 95). These stitches now form new edges of needlework and are your future seam lines.

Door sign

3. With right sides together, baste eyelet to Aida/lining, pivoting at corners. Start in middle of one side; turn back ¼" at start and finish. Overlap ends by 1". Get bottom of eyelet heading lined up on seam lines. Machine-stitch (Illus. 96). Use white thread. Check to see that eyelet lies correctly. Eyelet heading will be hidden in future seams.
4. Add ribbon to top of design. On right side of Aida combination, measure 1½" from top corners. Mark cloth with pins. With ends of ribbon extended 1" beyond eyelet heading and centered over pins, baste ribbon in place. Loop lies towards center of design (Illus. 97).
5. With right sides together, pin Aida combination over

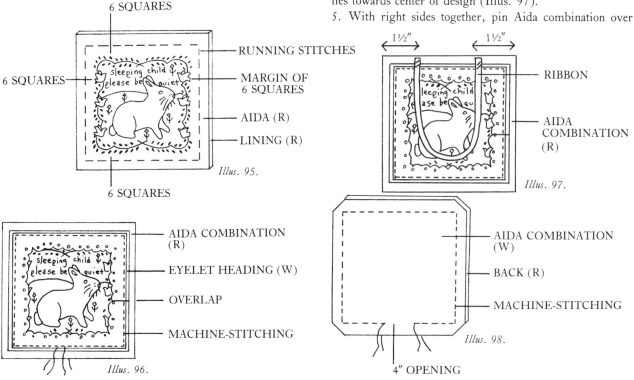

76

back with eyelet and ribbon wedged in between. Machine-stitch, using seam lines in Step 3 as your guide, pivoting at corners. Leave 4″ opening in middle of bottom. Trim seams to ⅝″. Slash corners on diagonal (Illus. 98).

6. Turn. Press opening in on seam line.

7. Push polyester fibre through opening in rectangle until it feels firm. Distribute evenly.

8. Close hole by slip-stitching.

CROSS-STITCH KEY (use two strands)

Symbol	J. & P. Coats	DMC
T	7976 Baby Blue	3325
O	3067 Baby Pink	963
=	5365 no name	435
♥	5471 Coffee Brown	433
⊠	6267 Avocado Green	469
▲	2326 Copper	920
◆	3127 Carnation Lt.	894
·	6250 Pine Green Lt.	772
□	Cloth as is	

BACKSTITCH KEY (use two strands)

Symbol	J. & P. Coats	DMC
	5471 Coffee Brown	433

Backstitch Area: 5471 Coffee Brown (or 433)—Everything.

Orange Calf *(In color on page F.) (Advanced.)*

Size: Embroidered rectangle approximately 14″ wide × 8½″.

Aida 11, white: Cut cloth 21″ wide × 18″.

Embroidery floss: Coats 4104 Lavender Dk. (or DMC 210), 6227 Christmas Green Bright (700), 6020 Nile Green (954), 8403 Black (310), 2330 Burnt Pumpkin (947), 2314 Tangerine Med. (741), 2326 Copper (920), 2292 Golden Yellow Very Lt. (3078), 2298 Canary Deep (972), 5471 Coffee Brown (433), 7022 Cornflower Blue Dk. (797), 6261 Avocado Green Med. (470), 3126 Melon Lt. (3326), and 4092 Violet Med. (553). Purchase one skein of each.

Other materials: Mint green cotton, for back, ⅜ yard. White cotton, for pillow insert, ⅜ yard. White pregathered cotton eyelet ruffle, 1¾″ wide × 1⅝ yards. Poly-fil 100% polyester fibre, approximately 9 ounces. Tracing paper.

Making the first cross-stitch: Measure across 4″ from top left corner; measure downwards 4¼″ from top left corner. Mark point where two measurements intersect. Refer to chart. Start sewing at arrow.

Personalizing pillow: On graph paper, plan baby's name, date of birth, weight, length, and place of birth. See alphabet and numbers provided. There are 119 spaces available for each of four lines. Name line illustrates exact placement for start and finish of information. Place each line in same position on chart with your facts centered. On line one include first, middle name or initial, and last name. On line two include birth date and words "born on" if information is short. On line three, include weight and length. If information is brief, add words such as "weight," "length," "pounds," or "ounces." On line four, include city and state. If city runs long, use postal abbreviations for state. Leave one space between each letter, between date and comma, between punctuation and number, and between punctuation and word. Leave five spaces between each complete word, between punctuation and dates, and between punctuation and words.

Finishing directions

1. Make pillow patterns for front, insert (Illus. 99), and back (Illus. 100).
2. With right sides up, place front pattern over embroidery. Arrange paper so borders on either side of design are equal (mine were 1″ each), and there is a 1⅜″ border at top of embroidery. Pin. Cut. Transfer markings to wrong side of fabric.
3. Lay out and cut patterns for back and insert. Transfer markings to wrong side of cloth.
4. Repeat Step 3 in "Rabbit." The only exception is: This project has Aida only.

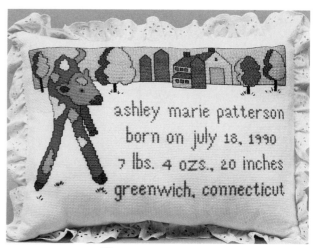

Birth announcement pillow

Illus. 99.

FRONT
CUT ONE EMBROIDERED AIDA
CUT TWO WHITE COTTON FOR INSERT

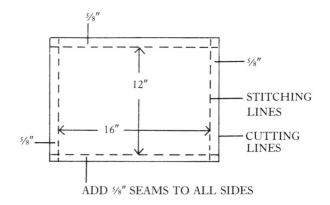

ADD ⅝″ SEAMS TO ALL SIDES

Illus. 100.

BACK
CUT TWO MINT GREEN COTTON

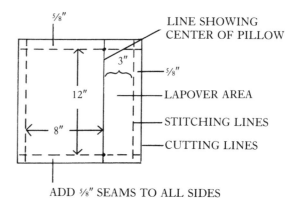

ADD ⅝″ SEAMS TO ALL SIDES

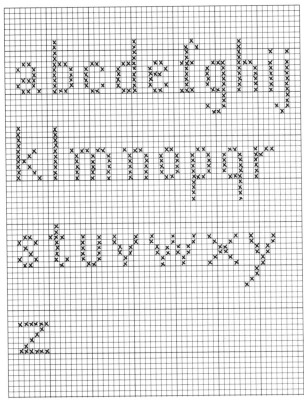

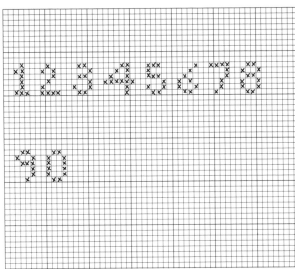

Extra letters and numbers

CROSS-STITCH KEY (use two strands)

Symbol	J. & P. Coats	DMC
·	4104 Lavender Dk.	210
e	6227 Christmas Green Bright	700
/	6020 Nile Green	954
◆	8403 Black	310
=	2330 Burnt Pumpkin	947
○	2314 Tangerine Med.	741
▲	2326 Copper	920
S	2292 Golden Yellow Very Lt.	3078
T	2298 Canary Deep	972
Z	5471 Coffee Brown	433
L	7022 Cornflower Blue Dk.	797
△	6261 Avocado Green Med.	470
C	3126 Melon Lt.	3326
⊠	4092 Violet Med.	553
□	Cloth as is	

BACKSTITCH KEY (use two strands)

Symbol	J. & P. Coats	DMC
	8403 Black	310

Backstitch Area: 8403 Black (or 310)—Everything.

5. Repeat Steps 12–14 in "Cyclamen." The only exceptions are: This project has eyelet instead of piping/ruffle, and at Step 14, you should use eyelet seam lines as your guide.
6. Turn pillow. Press.
7. With right sides together and seams matching, pin inserts together. Machine-stitch, leaving 5″ opening in middle of one side (Illus. 101).
8. Repeat Steps 6–8 in "Rabbit." The only exception is: In this project you are stuffing an insert and not the actual object.
9. Push insert through slit in back of pillow.

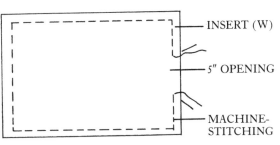

Illus. 101.

Chart on following page.

Farm Animals in Repeat *(In color on page I.)* *(Advanced.)*

Size: Embroidery approximately 19½" wide × 3¼".

Aida 11, white: Cut cloth 34" wide × 9½".

Embroidery floss: Coats 3000 Garnet (or DMC 815), 3281 Pink Med. (776), 7161 Blue Lt. (813), 5000 Russet (434), 3151 Cranberry Very Lt. (604), 7020 no name (800), 2293 Yellow Dark (744), 4303 Lavender Lt. (211), 6250 Pine Green Lt. (772), 8403 Black (310), and 5388 Beige (644). Purchase two skeins each of 3151 Cranberry Very Lt. (604), 4303 Lavender Lt. (211), and 8403 Black (310). Buy one skein of each remaining color.

Other materials: Stuffed animal, 15" tall, 21" at waist (waist should be between 18" and 21" and absolutely no larger than 21"), and 12" seated (Illus. 102). White pre-gathered cotton eyelet ruffle, 1" wide × ⅞ yard. Pink satin ribbon, double-faced, ⅝" wide × 1 yard. White elastic, ⅜" wide × ⅝ yard.

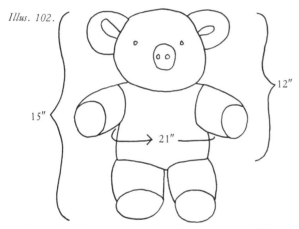

Illus. 102.

Making the first cross-stitch: Measure across 7" from left end of horizontally held cloth; measure downwards 3½" from top left corner. Mark point where two measurements intersect. Refer to chart. Start sewing at arrow.

Finishing directions

1. Before sewing skirt together, extend lavender, green, and black stripes by 5" on either side of original charted design (Illus. 103). This adds simple decoration to back of skirt.

Illus. 103.

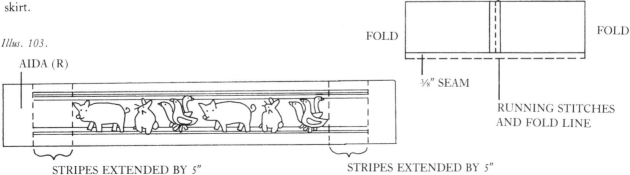

AIDA (R)

STRIPES EXTENDED BY 5"   STRIPES EXTENDED BY 5"

Stuffed animal skirt

2. With right sides together and stripes matching, machine-stitch across ends of Aida. Sew right next to embroidery. Trim seams to ⅝" (Illus. 104). Press open.

Illus. 104.

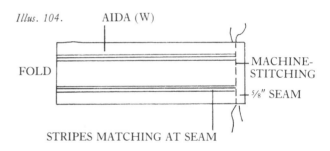

AIDA (W)

FOLD

MACHINE-STITCHING

⅝" SEAM

STRIPES MATCHING AT SEAM

3. From bottom of embroidery, count down margin of six squares on Aida. Mark cloth with pin. Using knotted single strand of thread, hand-stitch this line by following one row in Aida and by weaving in and out cloth with ½" running stitches. Press bottom of skirt towards wrong side of fabric on running stitches. Trim Aida to ⅜" beyond fold (Illus. 105).

BACK OF SKIRT (W)

Illus. 105.

CENTER SEAM

FOLD   FOLD

⅜" SEAM

RUNNING STITCHES AND FOLD LINE

4. Add eyelet to bottom of skirt. With right sides up and starting at back, place eyelet heading under folded edge of Aida. At start and finish turn back ¼″ of eyelet. Overlap ends by 1½″. Pin. Baste. On right side Aida, machine-stitch close to folded edge cloth (Illus. 106). Use white thread.

6. At top of skirt, make casing for elastic. On fold 2, press ¼″ seam allowance back towards wrong side fabric. Press Aida back again towards wrong side of fabric on fold 1. Pin. Machine-stitch close to edge of fold 2, leaving 2″ opening in back (Illus. 108).

Illus. 106.   BACK OF SKIRT (R)

CENTER SEAM

FOLD   FOLD

OVERLAP

MACHINE-STITCHING

Illus. 108.   BACK OF SKIRT (W)

MACHINE-STITCHING

FOLD 1

FOLD 2

FOLD   (R)   2″ OPENING   FOLD

OVERLAP

5. With right sides up, prepare top of skirt for completion. First, at top of embroidery, count up margin of eight squares on Aida. Mark cloth with pin. Using knotted single strand of white thread, hand-stitch this line by following one row in Aida and by weaving in and out cloth with ½″ running stitches. Call this line fold 1. Second, above fold 1 count up an additional margin of six squares. Mark cloth with pin. Hand-stitch this line as above. Call this fold 2. Trim fabric above fold 2 to ¼″ seam allowance (Illus. 107).

7. Measure animal's waist. Cut elastic 2½″ shorter than measurement.

8. Attach safety pin to one end of elastic. Slide safety pin combination through opening in casing. Overlap ends by 1″ and machine-stitch.

9. Machine-stitch opening in casing closed.

10. Center skirt on animal.

11. Tie bow at neck.

Illus. 107.   AIDA DETAIL (R)

CUT EDGE OF CLOTH

¼″ SEAM ALLOWANCE

FOLD 2

MARGIN OF 6 SQUARES

FOLD 1

MARGIN OF 8 SQUARES

EMBROIDERY

EYELET

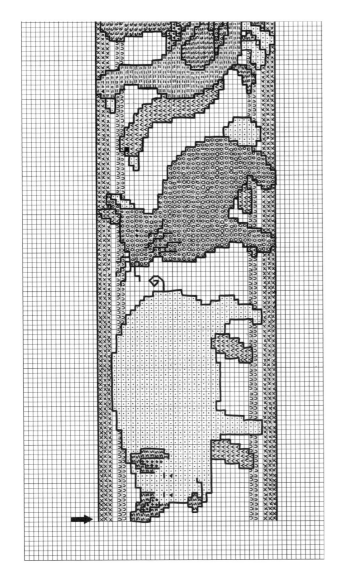

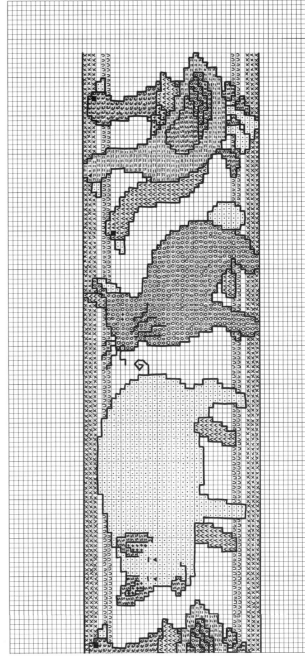

CROSS-STITCH KEY (use two strands)

Symbol	J. & P. Coats	DMC
◆	3000 Garnet	815
S	3281 Pink Med.	776
▲	7161 Blue Lt.	813
△	5000 Russet	434
·	3151 Cranberry Very Lt.	604
○	7020 no name	800
═	2293 Yellow Dark	744
⊠	4303 Lavender Lt.	211
U	6250 Pine Green Lt.	772
■	8403 Black	310
e	5388 Beige	644
☐	Cloth as is	

BACKSTITCH KEY (use two strands)

Symbol	J. & P. Coats	DMC
	8403 Black	310

Backstitch Area: 8403 Black (or 310)—Everything.

GIFTS FOR THE CAT FANCIER

My Pet *(In color on page P.)* *(Simple.)*

Size: Embroidery approximately 3⅜″ wide × 1⅝″.

Maxi-weave Ribband, 14-count, white with gold edging, 1⅞″ wide: Cut band 14″.

Embroidery floss: Coats 7030 Blue (or DMC 799), 2326 Copper (920), 8403 Black (310), 3125 Pink Med. (776), 5942 Tan Brown Lt. (437), and 5471 Coffee Brown (433). Purchase one skein of each.

Making the first cross-stitch: Measure across 2½″ from left end of horizontally held Ribband. Refer to chart. Start sewing at arrow.

Finishing directions

1. Finish off top end of bookmark. With right sides up, measure 1⅛″ beyond left edge of blue embroidery. Mark cloth with pin. Press back fabric. Add ½″ seam allowance beyond fold. Cut off excess Ribband (Illus. 109). Turn under ¼″ on raw edge. Press. Slip-stitch on folded inner edge (Illus. 110).

Bookmark

2. Finish off bottom. Repeat Step 1. The only exception is: Measure 6½″ beyond right edge of blue embroidery (Illus. 111).

Illus. 111.

RIBBAND (R)

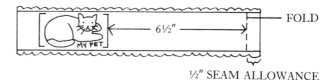

FOLD

½″ SEAM ALLOWANCE

Illus. 109.

RIBBAND (R)

FOLD

1⅛″

½″ SEAM ALLOWANCE

FOLD

FOLDED INNER EDGE

(R)

SLIP-STITCHING

RIBBAND (W)

Illus. 110.

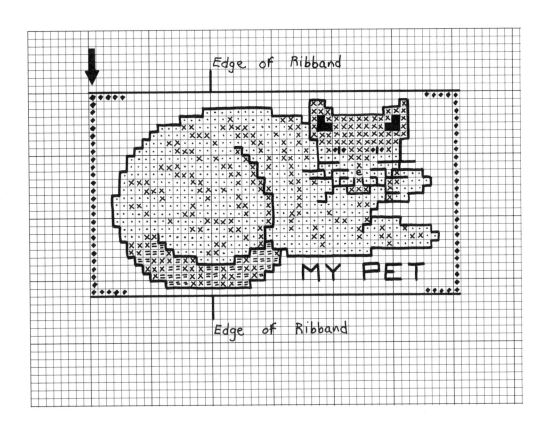

CROSS-STITCH KEY (use two strands)

Symbol	J. & P. Coats	DMC
◆	7030 Blue	799
⊠	2326 Copper	920
e	8403 Black	310
■	3125 Pink Med.	776
·	5942 Tan Brown Lt.	437
⊟	5471 Coffee Brown	433
□	Cloth as is	

BACKSTITCH KEY (use two strands)

Symbol	J. & P. Coats	DMC
	8403 Black	310

Backstitch Area: 8403 Black (or 310)—Everything.

Alternating Cat and Bird *(In color on page O.)* *(Simple.)*

Size: Band approximately 14″ wide × 1⅞″.

Maxi-weave Ribband, 14-count, white with pink edging, 1⅞″ wide: Cut band 18″.

Embroidery floss: Coats 8403 Black (or DMC 310), 3125 Pink Med. (776), 3128 Carnation Dk. (602), 6256 Parrot Green Med. (704), and 8512 Pewter Grey (317). Purchase one skein of each.

Other materials: Pink food container, 14″ in circumference, 4½″ in diameter, and 4⅝″ high (Illus. 112). Flat white cotton edging, ⅝″ wide × ⅞ yard. One fancy black plastic button, ¾″ in diameter (Illus. 113). White glue.

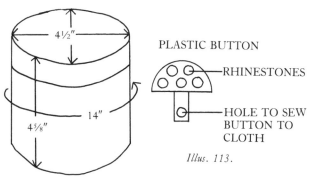

PLASTIC BUTTON

RHINESTONES

HOLE TO SEW BUTTON TO CLOTH

Illus. 113.

Illus. 112.

Making the first cross-stitch: Measure across 2¼″ from left end of horizontally held Ribband. See Step 1.

Finishing directions

1. If your container differs in size from mine, each embroidery repeat is approximately 3″ wide. Add or delete full repeats to fit your container. Refer to chart. Start sewing at arrow.

2. Center and glue button on top of lid. With point of scissors, make small hole in lid. Push button through hole so underside is level with cardboard. Remove button. Apply glue on bottom and reposition. Let dry.

Container band

3. Add trim to top and bottom of Ribband. With right sides up, place trim ¼″ beneath edges of Ribband. Pin. Baste. Cut trim same length as Ribband. Machine-stitch just inside pink edging (Illus. 114). Use white thread.

4. Place Ribband on container. Lap end over start. Turn back end of Ribband. Press. If fabric beyond fold is more than ¾″, cut off excess Ribband. Tightly rewrap band. Slip-stitch or glue ends together (Illus. 115).

TRIM (R)   MACHINE-STITCHING

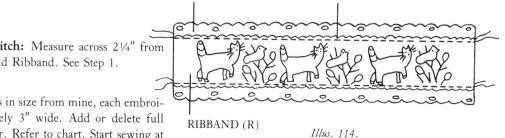

RIBBAND (R)   *Illus. 114.*

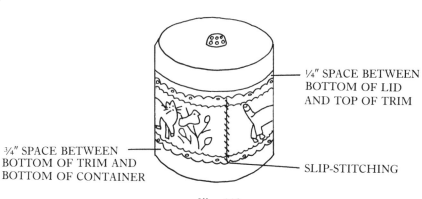

¼″ SPACE BETWEEN BOTTOM OF LID AND TOP OF TRIM

¾″ SPACE BETWEEN BOTTOM OF TRIM AND BOTTOM OF CONTAINER

SLIP-STITCHING

Illus. 115.

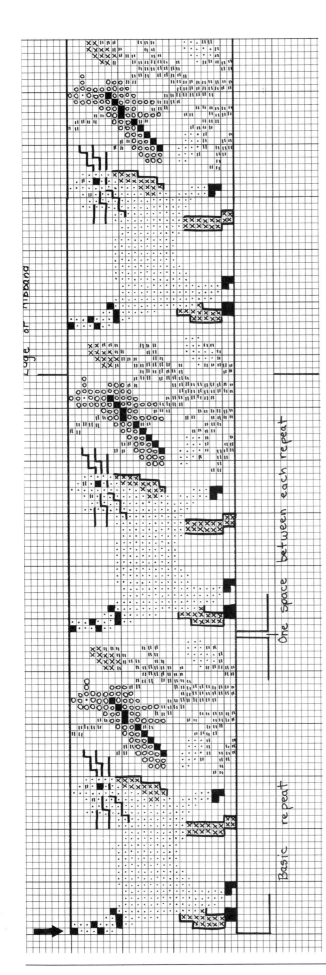

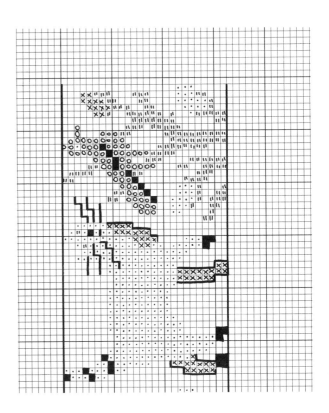

CROSS-STITCH KEY (use two strands)

Symbol	J. & P. Coats	DMC
■	8403 Black	310
⊠	3125 Pink Med.	776
·	3128 Carnation Dk.	602
≡	6256 Parrot Green Med.	704
⊡	8512 Pewter Grey	317
□	Cloth as is	

BACKSTITCH KEY (use two strands)

Symbol	J. & P. Coats	DMC
	8403 Black	310
	3128 Carnation Dk.	602

Backstitch Area: 8403 Black (or 310)—Cat's whiskers and mouth. 3128 Carnation Dk (or 602)—Cat's chest and two legs.

Shorthair Up Close *(In color on page M.)* *(Intermediate.)*

Size: Circle approximately 4⅞″ in diameter.

Aida 14, antique white: Cut cloth 9″ square.

Embroidery floss: Coats 8403 Black (or DMC 310), 1001 White (Snow-White), 3011 Coral (351), 5363 Old Gold Lt. (783), 5471 Topaz Very Ultra Dk. (433), 5365 no name (976), 6256 Parrot Green Med. (3347), 6228 Christmas Green (699), and 6250 Pine Green Lt. (772). Purchase one skein of each.

Other materials: Sudberry House Broider Box (woodstain with 5″ round design area, style #99041). Light gold nylon cording, ⅛″ wide × 18″. White glue.

Making the first cross-stitch: Measure across 4″ from top left corner; measure downwards 2″ from top left corner. Mark point where two measurements intersect. Refer to chart. Start sewing at arrow.

Finishing directions

1. With right side up, add ¾″ margin to edge of embroidered circle. With pencil and ruler, mark right side of cloth with dots at frequent intervals. Then using dots as your guide, machine-stitch a circle (Illus. 116).

Box lid

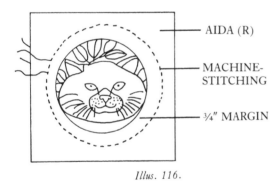

Illus. 116.

2. With sewing machine set for long basting stitches, stitch ¼″ to inside of first circle. Leave thread tails.
3. Cut Aida into a circle. To do, cut ⅛″ beyond first stitching (Illus. 117).

4. With wrong sides up, center mounting board over embroidered circle. Gather up Aida by pulling in on basting stitches (Illus. 118). At same time, stretch design to get edges of embroidery on edges of mounting board. Knot threads.
5. On back of Aida combination, put glue under gathered edges of fabric. As glue hardens, keep pressing Aida flat. Let dry.
6. Apply glue to back of Aida combination. Center in recessed lid. Put weight on top. Let dry.
7. Glue nylon cording over edges of Aida combination and in gap that exists between needlework and sides of wood. Start and end at cat's left shoulder. Butt ends together. As glue hardens, keep pressing cording in place. Let dry.

BACK VIEW

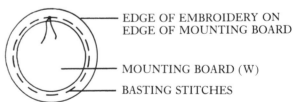

— EDGE OF EMBROIDERY ON EDGE OF MOUNTING BOARD

— MOUNTING BOARD (W)

— BASTING STITCHES

Illus. 118.

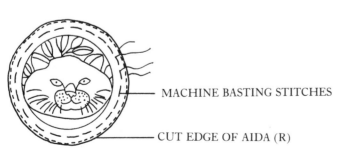

— MACHINE BASTING STITCHES

— CUT EDGE OF AIDA (R)

Illus. 117.

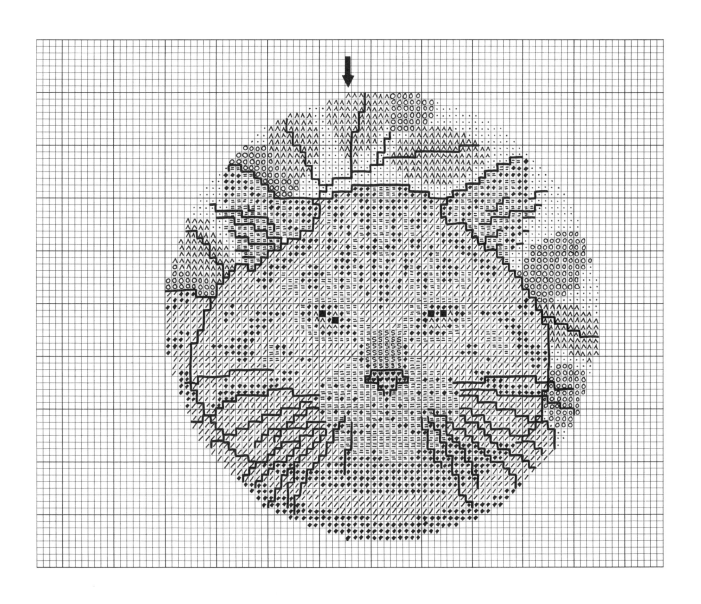

CROSS-STITCH KEY (use two strands)

Symbol	J. & P. Coats	DMC
◆	8403 Black	310
■	1001 White	Snow-White
♥	3011 Coral	351
=	5363 Old Gold Lt.	783
/	5471 Topaz Very Ultra Dk.	433
S	5365 no name	976
∧	6256 Parrot Green Med.	3347
○	6228 Christmas Green	699
·	6250 Pine Green Lt.	772
□	Cloth as is	

BACKSTITCH KEY (use two strands on black and green, use three strands on white)

Symbol	J. & P. Coats	DMC
	8403 Black	310
	6228 Christmas Green	699
	1001 White	Snow-White

Backstitch Area: 8403 Black (or 310)—Outline around face, ears, shoulders, nose, and lines within ears. 6228 Christmas Green (699)—Stems and veins within leaves. 1001 White (Snow-White)—Whiskers.

Among the Flowers *(In color on page M.)* *(Intermediate.)*

Size: Embroidery approximately 5⅝″ wide × 4⅝″.

Aida 14, white: Cut cloth 9½″ wide × 8½″.

Embroidery floss: Coats 8397 no name (or DMC 648), 8401 Steel Grey (646), 7030 Blue (799), 7020 no name (800), 2294 Topaz Lt. (726), 5363 Old Gold Lt. (783), 3127 Carnation Lt. (894), 8403 Black (310), 2314 Tangerine Med. (741), 4104 Lavender Dk. (210), 3067 Baby Pink (818), 6031 Emerald Green Dk. (910), and 6256 Parrot Green Med. (704). Purchase one skein of each.

Other materials: Commercially made notebook, 8¼″ wide × 10½″ high × ⅜″ deep (Illus. 119) with blue and white printed design. Unbleached muslin, for backing, 9½″ wide × 8½″. Stitch Witchery—9½″ wide × 8½″. Blue rickrack, ½″ wide × ¾ yard. White glue.

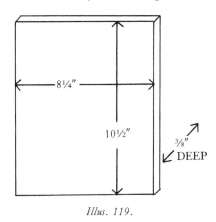

Illus. 119.

Making the first cross-stitch: Measure 2″ from top left corner; measure downwards 2″ from top left corner. Mark point where two measurements intersect. Refer to chart. Start sewing at arrow.

Finishing directions
1. Repeat Step 1 in "Horse and Rider."
2. Cut down Aida/Stitch Witchery/muslin. Count out margin of one square from all four sides of embroidery. Mark cloth with pins. Cut off excess cloth by following four rows in Aida that are next to pins.
3. With rights sides up, place Aida combination on notebook cover. Get margins equal at top and sides (mine were 1¼″). With pencil mark corners of Aida combination for future placement (Illus. 120).
4. Apply glue to back of Aida combination along edges and in center. With right sides up, place Aida combination on cover within penciled markings. Let dry.
5. With right sides up, glue rickrack just over edges of Aida combination. Start in middle of bottom. Overlap ends by ⅜″. At corners, turn rickrack over to other side, and continue going in new direction (Illus. 121). As glue hardens, keep pressing rickrack in place.

Notebook cover

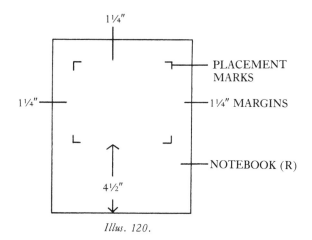

Illus. 120.

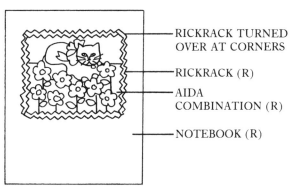

Illus. 121.

Cross-Stitch Key on following page.

CROSS-STITCH KEY (use two strands)

Symbol	J. & P. Coats	DMC
·	8397 no name	648
e	8401 Steel Grey	646
o	7030 Blue	799
=	7020 no name	800
T	2294 Topaz Lt.	726
△	5363 Old Gold Lt.	783
U	3127 Carnation Lt.	894
■	8403 Black	310
S	2314 Tangerine Med.	741
L	4104 Lavender Dk.	210
▲	3067 Baby Pink	818
◆	6031 Emerald Green Dk.	910
⊠	6256 Parrot Green Med.	704
☐	Cloth as is	

BACKSTITCH KEY (use two strands)

Symbol	J. & P. Coats	DMC
	8403 Black	310

Backstitch Area: 8403 Black (or 310)—Everything.

Tangled Yarn *(In color on page M.) (Intermediate.)*

Tray

Size: Three circles each approximately 3¾″ in diameter.

Aida 14, blue: Cut cloth into three 6″ squares.

Embroidery floss: Coats 2326 Copper (or DMC 920), 5472 Coffee Brown Med. (801), 5942 Tan Brown Lt. (437), 7010 Imperial Blue (995), 7161 Blue Lt. (813), 7181 Blue Dk. (825), 8403 Black (310), and 3072 Christmas Red Med. (816). Purchase one skein of each for set.

Other materials: Sudberry House Snack Tray (woodstain with set of three 3½″ round designs) or three Sudberry Coaster/Ash Trays (woodstain with 3½″ round designs, style #15751). Unbleached muslin, for backing, three 6″ squares. Stitch Witchery, three 6″ squares. Tracing paper. White glue.

Making the first cross-stitch: For left side of design, measure across 2⅜″ from top left corner; measure downwards 1⅞″ from top left corner. For center design, measure across 2″ from top left corner; measure downwards 1¾″. For right side of design, measure across 3″ from top left corner; measure downwards 1⅞″. Mark points where two measurements intersect. Refer to charts. Start sewing at arrows.

Finishing directions

1. Remove cardboard backings from tray. Apply glue to wrong side of each circle. Center and reset.

2. On three embroidered squares, repeat Step 1 in "Horse and Rider."

3. With right sides up, place tracing paper over one hole in tray. Trace around outer edges of hole. Fold circle in half and then in quarters. Open circle. Cut out (Illus. 122).

4. With right sides up, place tracing paper pattern over one design. Use quarter folds in circle as guidelines to center pattern on Aida/Stitch Witchery/muslin. Pin. Cut Aida combination to size of pattern. Repeat procedure with two remaining designs.

5. Add dab of glue to back of each Aida combination. With right sides up, press each design in tray. Let dry. Add glass.

Illus. 122.

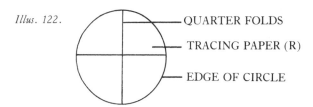

QUARTER FOLDS

TRACING PAPER (R)

EDGE OF CIRCLE

Chart and Cross-Stitch Key on following page.

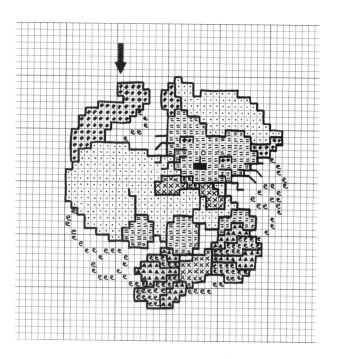

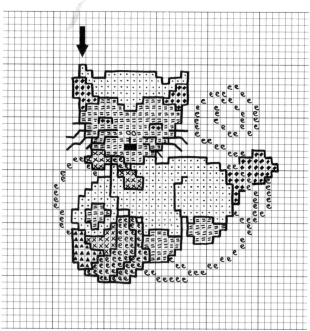

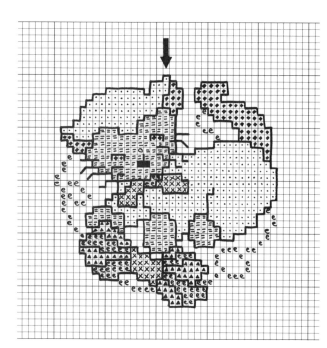

CROSS-STITCH KEY (use two strands)

Symbol	J. & P. Coats	DMC
·	2326 Copper	920
◆	5472 Coffee Brown Med.	801
═	5942 Tan Brown Lt.	437
▲	7010 Imperial Blue	995
e	7161 Blue Lt.	813
⊠	7181 Blue Dk.	825
○	8403 Black	310
■	3072 Christmas Red Med.	816
☐	Cloth as is	

BACKSTITCH KEY (use two strands)

Symbol	J. & P. Coats	DMC
	8403 Black	310

Backstitch Area: 8403 Black (or 310)—Everything.

The "Rabbit" door sign is on page 78, and "Farm Animals in Repeat," the stuffed animal's skirt, is on page 81.

I

J

Facing page: wall plaques—(top) "1064 Palmetto Street," page 108, and (bottom) "351 Oakleigh Street," page 106.

Above: "1511 Church Street" wall plaque, page 112.

The "Dove" Valentine card (top) is on page 38, and the "Peace" Christmas card is on page 18. There are two types of coordinated place mats and napkins: "Snowman's Set" on page 22 and "Interlocking Heart Set" on page 34.

Left: "Shorthair Up Close" box lid on page 90, "Among the Flowers" notebook cover on page 92, and "Tangled Yarn" tray on page 95.

Below: "Folk Art Set," coordinated pot holders and towel, on page 61; "Fruit and Ivy" pot holder on page 46; and "Mirrored Hearts" plant tub on page 36.

The "Chickens" bread cover is on page 52, and the "Hearts and Lillies" runner is on page 42.

The "Siamese Red Point" wall plaque is on page 99, and the "Alternating Cat and Bird" container band is on page 88.

I LIKE LITTLE KITTY, HER
COAT IS SO WARM, AND IF
I DON'T HURT HER, SHE'LL
DO ME NO HARM.

FOR A
WONDERFUL
DAD

HAPPY FATHER'S DAY

Clockwise: "Kitten with Toys" wall hanging on page 101, "Blue Cat" container on page 97, "My Pet" bookmark on page 86, and "Horse and Rider" wall plaque on page 50.

Blue Cat *(In color on page P.) (Intermediate.)*

Size: Embroidered rectangle approximately 6⅞" wide × 3⅛".

Perforated paper, 14-count ivory: Cut paper 7" wide × 4⅛".

Embroidery floss: Coats 7022 Cornflower Blue Dk. (or DMC 798), 7001 Peacock Blue (995), 7159 Blue Very Lt. (827), 2294 Topaz Lt. (726), 3151 Cranberry Very Lt. (605), 8403 Black (310), and 3046 Christmas Red Bright (666). Purchase two skeins of 7022 Cornflower Blue Dk. (798). Buy one skein of each remaining color.

Other materials: Unfinished wooden washboard with small container at bottom (outer dimensions of 7⅜" wide × 13¾" with recessed design area of 6⅞" wide × 3⅛" (Illus. 123)). Red soutache braid, ⅛" wide × 20". Brown Kiwi Shoe Polish (paste). Sawtooth picture hanger. Tracing paper. White glue.

Making the first cross-stitch: Measure across 1⅛" from top left corner; measure downwards ¹¹⁄₁₆" from top left corner. Mark point where two measurements intersect. Refer to chart. Start sewing at arrow.

Finishing directions

1. Apply polish to front, sides, and back of wood. Apply four to five coats to create a medium brown color. To do, apply shoe polish, rub with rag or brush, and let dry. Repeat.

2. On your washboard, measure width and height of recessed design area (mine is 6⅞" wide × 3⅛"). Cut tracing paper same size.

3. With right sides up, center tracing paper pattern over perforated paper. Get sides and then top and bottom margins equal on cat design. Hold tracing paper still. Cut perforated paper same size.

4. Apply glue along back edges of perforated paper and in center under cat. With right sides up, press design in top of washboard. Let dry.

5. Glue soutache over edges of perforated paper. Start in middle of bottom. Butt ends together. As glue hardens, keep pressing soutache over edges of paper.

6. Center sawtooth picture hanger along top back edge of washboard.

Chart and Cross-Stitch Key on following page.

Pencil and notepad container

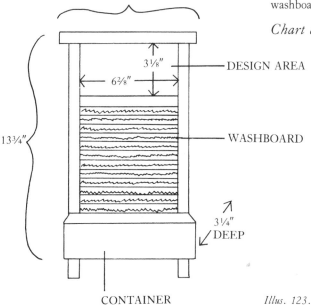

Illus. 123.

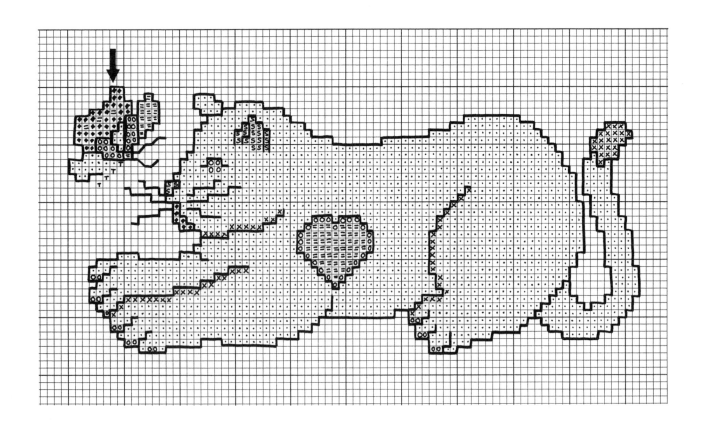

CROSS-STITCH KEY (use two strands)

Symbol	J. & P. Coats	DMC
·	7022 *Cornflower Blue Dk.*	798
◆	7001 *Peacock Blue*	995
⊠	7159 *Blue Very Lt.*	827
⊡	2294 *Topaz Lt.*	726
Ⓢ	3151 *Cranberry Very Lt.*	605
Ⓣ	8403 *Black*	310
⊟	3046 *Christmas Red Bright*	666
☐	*Paper as is*	

BACKSTITCH KEY (use two strands)

Symbol	J. & P. Coats	DMC
	8403 *Black*	310

Backstitch Area: 8403 Black (or 310)—Everything.

Siamese Red Point *(In color on page O.)* *(Advanced.)*

Size: Embroidery approximately 7⅞″ square.

Aida 11, ivory: Cut cloth 11½″ wide × 12″.

Embroidery floss: Coats 7021 Delft (or DMC 809), 3019 Rose Very Deep (use Coats color), 5363 Old Gold Lt. (use Coats color), 1001 White (Snow-White), 5388 Beige (644), 3067 Baby Pink (use Coats color), 3127 Carnation Lt. (894), use DMC color (611), 7023 Blue Med. (797), and 5471 Coffee Brown (433). Purchase two skeins each of 7021 Delft (809) and 5363 Old Gold Lt. (use Coats color). Buy one skein of each remaining color.

Other materials: Basswood Tavern Sign by Walnut Hollow Farm (unfinished wood with outer dimensions of 8″ wide × 12″, recessed design area of 8″ square (Illus. 124), style #5341). Unbleached muslin, for lining, 11″ square. White mat board, two 10″ squares. Dark brown suede or nylon cording, ⅛″ wide × 1 yard. Brown Kiwi Shoe Polish (paste). Sawtooth picture hanger. White glue.

WALL PLAQUE (R)

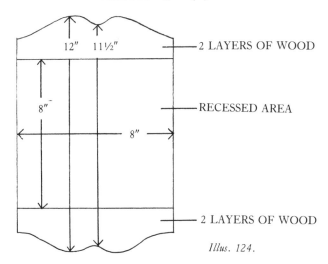

Illus. 124.

Making the first cross-stitch: Measure across 2″ from top left corner; measure downwards 2″ from top left corner. Mark point where two measurements intersect. Refer to chart. Start sewing at arrow.

Finishing directions

1. Repeat Step 1 in "Blue Cat."
2. On your plaque, measure width and height of recessed area (mine is 8″ square). Since cat is mounted over combination of mat board/muslin and edged in suede, subtract ⅛″ from each measurement so that design will fit in tight space (Illus. 125). Cut two pieces of mat board same size.
3. If your plaque is flat and does not have a recessed area, cut two pieces of mat board same size as embroidery.
4. Stack mat boards together. Tape in a north-south-east-west position.

Wall plaque

5. Center muslin over mat board. On back, stretch and fold in top and bottom. Tape. Stretch and fold in sides. Tape.
6. Repeat Steps 7–10 in "Mounting and Framing." The only exception is: At Step 7 there is no batting.
7. Glue brown suede on edges of Aida combination. Start in middle of bottom. Butt ends together. As glue hardens keep pressing suede on Aida.
8. On back of Aida combination, spread glue in four corners. With right sides up, center Aida combination in recessed area (if you have it) or flat on plaque. Put weight on top. Let dry.
9. Center sawtooth picture hanger along top back edge of plaque.

Chart and Cross-Stitch Key on following page.

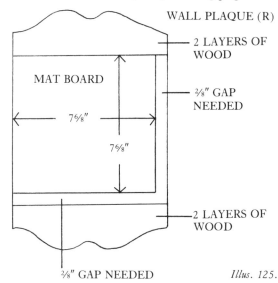

WALL PLAQUE (R)

— 2 LAYERS OF WOOD

MAT BOARD

— ⅛″ GAP NEEDED

7⅞″

7⅞″

— 2 LAYERS OF WOOD

⅛″ GAP NEEDED

Illus. 125.

CROSS-STITCH KEY (use two strands)

Symbol	J. & P. Coats	DMC
⊡	7021 Delft	809
◆	3019 Rose Very Deep	Use J. & P. Coats color
·	5363 Old Gold Lt.	Use J. & P. Coats color
=	1001 White	Snow-White
∧	5388 Beige	644
⊠	3067 Baby Pink	Use J. & P. Coats color
■	3127 Carnation Lt.	894
▲	Use DMC color	611
T	7023 Blue Med.	797
e	5471 Coffee Brown	433
☐	Cloth as is	

BACKSTITCH KEY (use two strands)

Symbol	J. & P. Coats	DMC
	5471 Coffee Brown	433

Backstitch Area: 5471 Coffee Brown (or 433)—Everything.

Kitten with Toys *(In color on page P.)* *(Challenging.)*

Wall hanging

Quote: *I Like Little Pussy*. Jane Taylor. In line one I substituted word "kitty" for "pussy."

Size: Embroidery approximately 13⅝″ wide × 12⅜″.

Aida 11, white: Cut cloth 19″ wide × 18½″.

Embroidery floss: Coats 2294 Topaz Lt. (or DMC 743), 8403 Black (310), 3067 Baby Pink (963), 2326 Copper (920), 7159 Blue Very Lt. (827), 5942 Tan Brown Lt. (437), 5471 Coffee Brown (433), and 7022 Cornflower Blue Dk. (798). Purchase three skeins of 5471 Coffee Brown (433) and two skeins each of 8403 Black (310) and 2326 Copper (920). Buy one skein of each remaining color.

Other materials: Custom frame.

Making the first cross-stitch: Measure across 3″ from top left corner; measure downwards 3″ from top left corner. Mark point where two measurements intersect. Refer to chart. Start sewing at arrow.

Finishing directions
1. See "Mounting and Framing."
2. Margin to be added at mounting: Add ¹³⁄₁₆″.

Chart and Cross-Stitch Key on following pages.

I LIKE LITTLE KITT[Y]
COAT IS SO WARM. A[ND]
I DON'T HURT HER.
DO ME NO HARM.

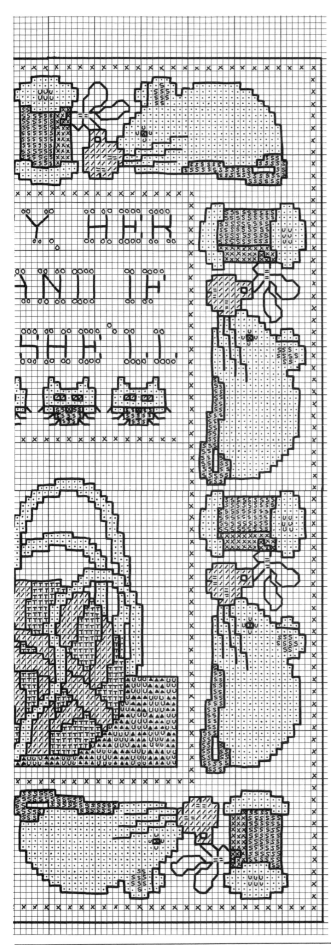

CROSS-STITCH KEY (use two strands)

Symbol	J. & P. Coats	DMC
∕	2294 Topaz Lt.	743
═	8403 Black	310
S	3067 Baby Pink	963
⊠	2326 Copper	920
U	7159 Blue Very Lt.	827
T	5942 Tan Brown Lt.	437
·	5471 Coffee Brown	433
▲	7022 Cornflower Blue Dk.	798
☐	Cloth as is	

BACKSTITCH KEY (use two strands)

Symbol	J. & P. Coats	DMC
	2326 Copper	920
	7022 Cornflower Blue Dk.	798
	8403 Black	310

Backstitch Area: 2326 Copper (or 920)—Rectangular outer border. 7022 Cornflower Blue Dk. (798)—Lines within lettering. 8403 Black (310)—Everything else.

HEIRLOOM GIFTS

351 Oakleigh Street *(In color on page J.)* *(Challenging.)*

Wall plaque

Size: Embroidery approximately 8½″ wide × 6½″.

Aida 11, ivory: Cut cloth 14″ wide × 11½″.

Embroidery floss: Coats 5371 Topaz Very Ultra Dk. (or DMC 435), 5472 Coffee Brown Med. (801), use DMC color (610), 8403 Black (310), 1001 White (Snow-White), 2293 Yellow Dark (743), 5363 Old Gold Lt. (use Coats color), 6211 Jade Very Dk. (991), 8401 Steel Grey (318), 6266 Apple Green (3347), 6239 Parrot Green Dk. (702), and 6030 Nile Green Lt. (954). Purchase two skeins each of 8403 Black (310) and 6266 Apple Green (3347). Buy one skein of each remaining color.

Other materials: Custom frame.

Making the first cross-stitch: Measure across 2½″ from top left corner; measure downwards 2½″ from top left corner. Mark point where two measurements intersect. Refer to chart. Start sewing at arrow.

Finishing directions

1. See "Mounting and Framing."
2. Margin to be added at mounting: Add ¾″.

CROSS-STITCH KEY (use two strands)

Symbol	J. & P. Coats	DMC
⊙	5371 Topaz Very Ultra Dk.	435
■	5472 Coffee Brown Med.	801
T	Use DMC color	610
=	8403 Black	310
∕	1001 White	Snow-White
S	2293 Yellow Dark	743
△	5363 Old Gold Lt.	Use J. & P. Coats color
◆	6211 Jade Very Dk.	991
U	8401 Steel Grey	318
L	6266 Apple Green	3347
3	6239 Parrot Green Dk.	702
·	6030 Nile Green Lt.	954
□	Cloth as is	

BACKSTITCH KEY (use two strands)

Symbol	J. & P. Coats	DMC
	8403 Black	310

Backstitch Area: 8403 Black (or 310)—Everything.

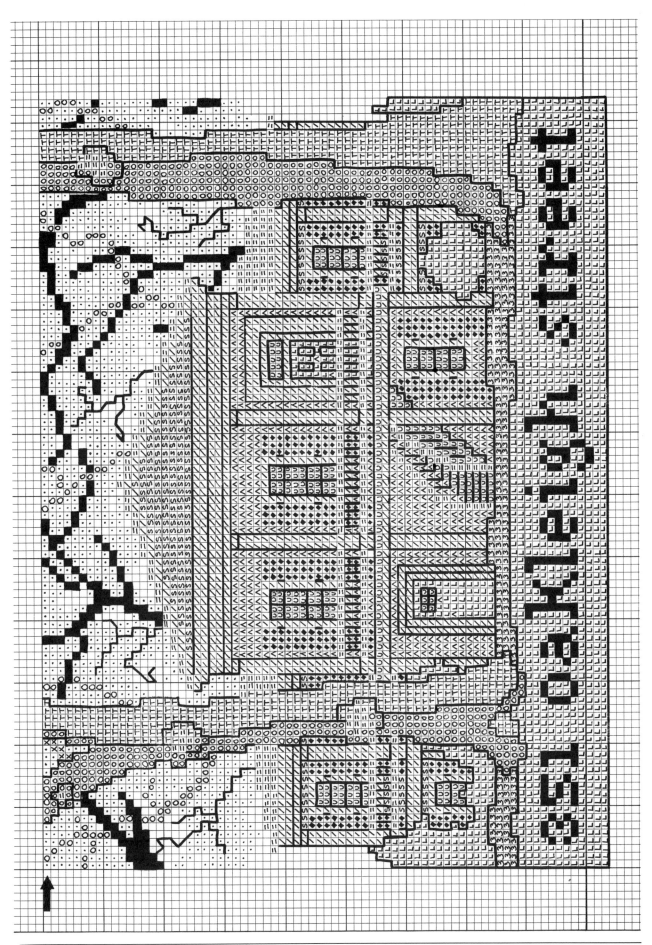

1064 Palmetto Street *(In color on page J.)* *(Challenging.)*

Wall plaque

Size: Embroidery approximately 10″ wide × 9¼″.

Aida 11, white: Cut cloth 16″ wide × 15″.

Embroidery floss: Coats 8403 Black (or DMC 310), 1001 White (Snow-White), use DMC color (646), 7021 Delft (809), 7030 Blue (799), 8399 Steel Grey Lt. (318), 2292 Golden Yellow Very Lt. (3078), 5365 no name (436), 5471 Coffee Brown (801), use DMC color (919), 2326 Copper (921), 5363 Old Gold Lt. (use Coats color), 7023 Blue Med. (797), 3046 Christmas Red Bright (666), 5942 Tan Brown Lt. (437), 6256 Parrot Green Med. (use Coats color), 6211 Jade Very Dk. (561), use DMC color (369), use DMC color (775), use DMC color (762), and 3021 Christmas Red Dk. (484). Purchase two skeins each of 8403 Black (310), 7021 Delft (809), and 6211 Jade Very Dk. (561). Buy one skein of each remaining color.

Other materials: Custom frame.

Making the first cross-stitch: Measure across 6″ from top left corner; measure downwards 3⅛″ from top left corner. Mark point where two measurements intersect. Refer to chart. Start sewing at arrow.

Finishing directions
1. See "Mounting and Framing."
2. Margin to be added at mounting: None. Use edges of embroidery as actual edges of design.

CROSS-STITCH KEY (use two strands)

Symbol	J. & P. Coats	DMC
⊠	8403 Black	310
·	1001 White	Snow-White
▣	Use DMC color	646
⊟	7021 Delft	809
T	7030 Blue	799
▲	8399 Steel Grey Lt.	318
■	2292 Golden Yellow Very Lt.	3078
⧄	5365 no name	436
C	5471 Coffee Brown	801
N	Use DMC color	919
L	2326 Copper	921
3	5363 Old Gold Lt.	Use J. & P. Coats color
◪	7023 Blue Med.	797
♥	3046 Christmas Red Bright	666
I	5942 Tan Brown Lt.	437
e	6256 Parrot Green Med.	Use J. & P. Coats color
S	6211 Jade Very Dk.	561
⦂	Use DMC color	369
U	Use DMC color	775
◆	Use DMC color	762
■	3021 Christmas Red Dk.	498
☐	Cloth as is	

BACKSTITCH KEY (use two strands)

Symbol	J. & P. Coats	DMC
	1001 White	Snow-White
	8403 Black	310

Backstitch Area: 1001 White (or Snow-White)—Lines within black windows. 8403 Black (310)—Everything else.

Chart on following pages.

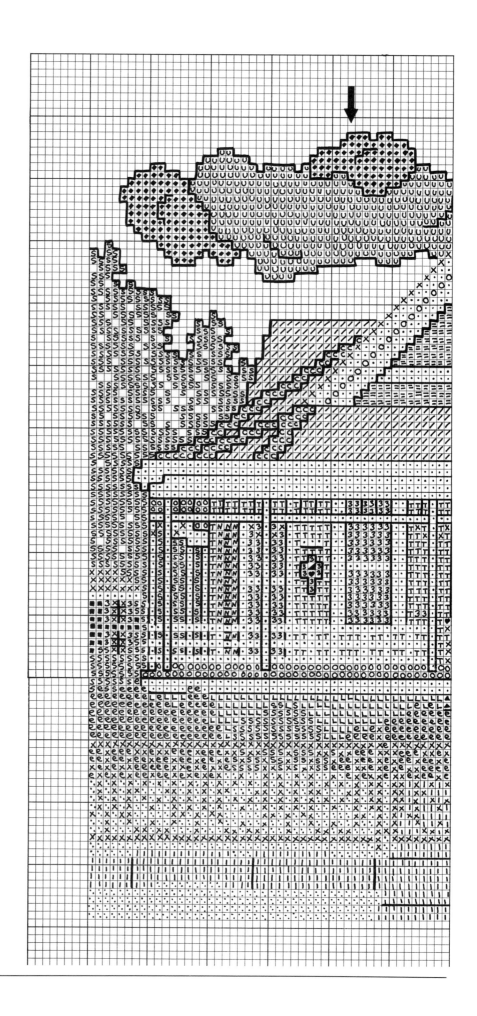

111

1511 Church Street *(In color on page K.)* *(Challenging.)*

Wall plaque

Size: Embroidery approximately 10″ wide × 7″.

Aida 11, ivory: Cut cloth 16″ wide × 13″.

Embroidery floss: Coats 1001 White (or DMC Snow-White), use DMC color (3371), use DMC color (422), use DMC color (3041), 5365 Old Gold Lt. (435), 6211 Jade Very Dk. (561), use DMC color (3405), 8401 Steel Grey (318), 5470 no name (434), 5472 Coffee Brown Med. (898), 6239 Parrot Green Dk. (702), 6001 Parrot Green Lt. (907), 8397 no name (3024), 6228 Christmas Green (699), 2326 Copper (921), 6266 Apple Green (use Coats color), and 5471 Coffee Brown (433). Purchase two skeins of White or use DMC color (3371). Buy one skein of each remaining color.

Other materials: Custom frame.

Making the first cross-stitch: Measure across 3⅜″ from top left corner; measure downwards 3″ from top left corner. Mark point where two measurements intersect. Refer to chart. Start sewing at arrow.

Finishing directions
1. See "Mounting and Framing."
2. Margin to be added at mounting: Add 1⅛″.

CROSS-STITCH KEY (use two strands)

Symbol	J. & P. Coats	DMC
⊟	1001 White	Snow-White
T	Use DMC color	3371
△	Use DMC color	422
·	Use DMC color	3041
◎	5365 Old Gold Lt.	435
⧄	6211 Jade Very Dk.	561
e	Use DMC color	3405
C	8401 Steel Grey	318
U	5470 no name	434
L	5472 Coffee Brown Med.	898
♥	6239 Parrot Green Dk.	702
▲	6001 Parrot Green Lt.	907
⋁	8397 no name	3024
Q	6228 Christmas Green	699
◆	2326 Copper	921
⊠	6266 Apple Green	Use J. & P. Coats color
S	5471 Coffee Brown	433
☐	Cloth as is	

BACKSTITCH KEY (use two strands)

Symbol	J. & P. Coats	DMC
	Use DMC color	3371

Backstitch Area: Use DMC color (3371)—Everything.

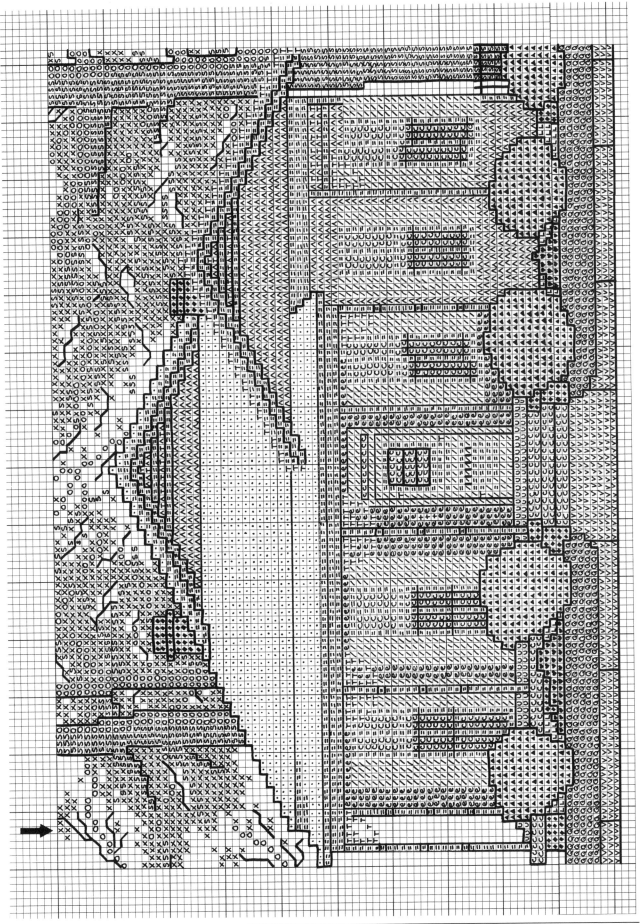

Shells *(In color on page A.)* *(Challenging.)*

Serving tray

Size: Embroidery approximately 13¼" wide × 7¼".

Aida 11, ivory: Cut cloth 19" wide × 12".

Embroidery floss: Coats 5360 Beige Brown Very Dk. (or DMC 838), 2326 Copper (921), 2337 Terra Cotta Lt. (754), 5365 no name (435), 5471 Coffee Brown (801), 5388 Beige (use Coats color), 5347 no name (use Coats color), 5942 Tan Brown Lt. (437), use DMC color (355), use DMC color (646), 1001 White (Snow-White), use DMC color (739), and 5470 no name (433). Purchase three skeins of 5470 no name (433). Purchase two skeins each of 5360 Beige Brown Very Dk. (838), 5942 Tan Brown Lt. (437), and use DMC color (739). Buy one skein of each remaining color.

Other materials: Classic Tray by Sudberry House (woodstain with 15½" × 8½" opening in rectangle mat, style #60101). Unbleached muslin, for backing, 19" wide × 12". Stitch Witchery, 19" wide × 12".

Making the first cross-stitch: Measure across 3¼" from top left corner; measure downwards 2¼" from top left corner. Mark point where two measurements intersect. Refer to chart. Start sewing at arrow.

Finishing directions
1. Repeat Step 1 in "Horse and Rider."
2. Remove screws at one end of tray. Slide out rectangle mat, cardboard, and base. Glass is inside. Handle with care; clean.
3. With rights sides up, center rectangle mat over Aida/Stitch Witchery/muslin. Get margins equal at sides (mine were about ⅝"). Cut off fabric that extends beyond mat.
4. Reassemble frame. Working from bottom to top, slide in base (wrong side up), cardboard, Aida combination (right side up), rectangle mat (right side up), and glass.
5. Replace end of tray.

CROSS-STITCH KEY (use two strands)

Symbol	J. & P. Coats	DMC
◆	5360 Beige Brown Very Dk.	838
▣	2326 Copper	921
⊠	2337 Terra Cotta Lt.	754
Ⓤ	5365 no name	435
Ⓛ	5471 Coffee Brown	801
Ⓢ	5388 Beige	Use J. & P. Coats color
Ⓩ	5347 no name	Use J. & P. Coats color
▣	5942 Tan Brown Lt.	437
△	Use DMC color	355
ⓔ	Use DMC color	646
■	1001 White	Snow-White
Ⓣ	Use DMC color	739
·	5470 no name	433
☐	Cloth as is	

BACKSTITCH KEY (use two strands)

Symbol	J. & P. Coats	DMC
	5360 Beige Brown Very Dk.	838

Backstitch Area: 5360 Beige Brown Very Dk. (or 838)— Everything.

Chart on following pages.

Hawaii One *(In color on page D.) (Challenging.)*

Coordinated wall hanging, left panel

Size: Embroidery approximately 15⅝″ wide × 9¾″.

Aida 11, white: Cut cloth 22″ wide × 16½″.

Embroidery floss: Coats 7022 Cornflower Blue Dk. (or DMC 797), 8403 Black (310), 7020 no name (800), 2326 Copper (920), 3067 Baby Pink (818), 2294 Topaz Lt. (726), 8514 Pewter Grey Dk. (413), 5943 Tan Brown (437), 2300 Yellow Beige Lt. (3047), 7030 Blue (799), 8510 Pearl Grey Very Lt. (762), 5472 Coffee Brown Med. (801), 8401 Steel Grey (318), 5363 Old Gold Lt. (use Coats color), 5365 no name (435), and 5471 Coffee Brown (433). Purchase four skeins of 8403 Black (310) and two skeins each of 8514 Pewter Grey Dk. (413), 8510 Pewter Grey Very Lt. (762), and 5363 Old Gold Lt. (use Coats color). Buy one skein of each remaining color.

Other materials: Custom frame.

Making the first cross-stitch: Measure across 3″ from top left corner; measure downwards 3″ from top left corner. Mark point where two measurements intersect. Refer to chart. Start sewing at arrow.

Finishing directions
1. See "Mounting and Framing."
2. Margin to be added at mounting: Add ⅞″.

Cross-Stitch Key on page 119, and chart on pages 120 and 121.

Hawaii Two *(In color on page D.) (Challenging.)*

Coordinated wall hanging, right panel

Size: Embroidery approximately 15⅝" wide × 9¾".

Aida 11, white: Cut cloth 22" wide × 16½".

Embroidery floss: Coats 7022 Cornflower Blue Dk. (or DMC 797), 8403 Black (310), 7020 no name (800), 2326 Copper (920), 3067 Baby Pink (818), 2294 Topaz Lt. (726), 8514 Pewter Grey Dk. (413), 5943 Tan Brown (437), 2300 Yellow Beige Lt. (3047), 7030 Blue (799), 8510 Pearl Grey Very Lt. (762), 5472 Coffee Brown Med. (801), 8401 Steel Grey (318), 5363 Old Gold Lt. (use Coats color), 5365 no name (435), and 5471 Coffee Brown (433). Purchase three skeins each of 8403 Black (310) and 5471 Coffee Brown (433). Purchase two skeins each of 8514 Pewter Grey Dk. (413), 8401 Steel Grey (318), 5363 Old Gold Lt. (use Coats color), and 5365 no name (435). Buy one skein of each remaining color.

Other materials: Custom frame.

Making the first cross-stitch: Measure across 3" from top left corner; measure downwards 3" from top left corner. Mark point where two measurements intersect. Refer to chart. Start sewing at arrow.

Finishing directions
1. See "Mounting and Framing."
2. Margin to be added at mounting: Add ⅞".

CROSS-STITCH KEY (use two strands)

Symbol	J. & P. Coats	DMC
▣	7022 Cornflower Blue Dk.	797
·	8403 Black	310
T	7020 no name	800
╱	2326 Copper	920
e	3067 Baby Pink	818
z	2294 Topaz Lt.	726
o	8514 Pewter Grey Dk.	413
s	5943 Tan Brown	437
◆	2300 Yellow Beige Lt.	3047
■	7030 Blue	799
⊠	8510 Pearl Grey Very Lt.	762
3	5472 Coffee Brown Med.	801
△	8401 Steel Grey	318
▤	5363 Old Gold Lt.	Use J. & P. Coats color
♥	5365 no name	435
▲	5471 Coffee Brown	433
☐	Cloth as is	

BACKSTITCH KEY (use two strands)

Symbol	J. & P. Coats	DMC
	8403 Black	310

Backstitch Area: 8403 Black (or 310)—Everything.

Chart on pages 122 and 123.

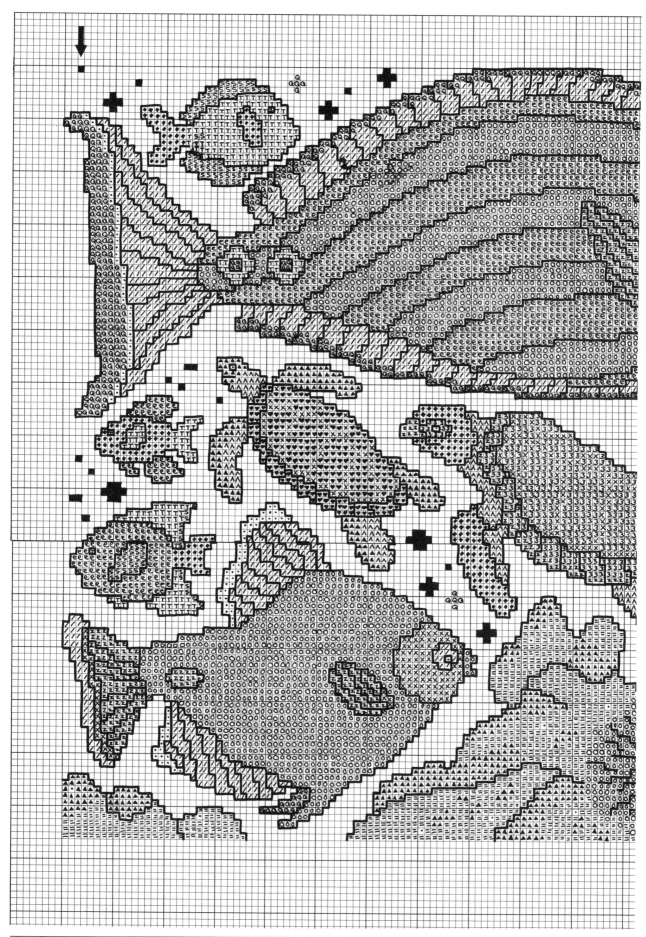

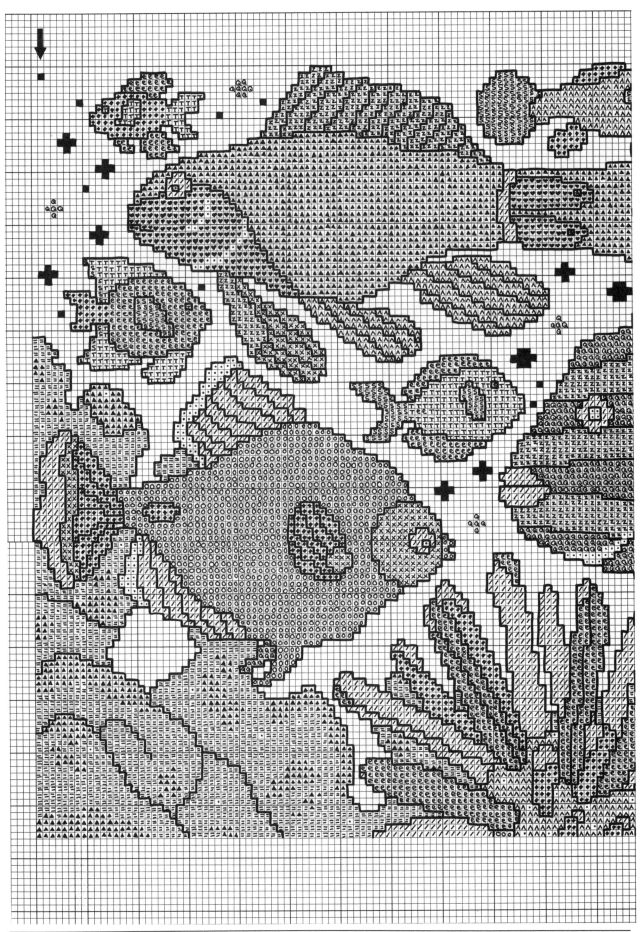

123

MOUNTING AND
FRAMING

Materials and Techniques

White Mat Board.
100% Polyester Batting.
Unbleached Muslin.
One-Inch Masking Tape.
White Six-Strand Embroidery Floss.
Regular Sewing Thread.
Ruler.
Mat Knife.
Pliers.
Large Crewel Needle.
Straight Pins.

In the few projects that require mounting and framing, there is a heading called "Margin to be added at mounting." It is here that you are asked to add a specified margin (¾" to 1½") to all four sides of the design before the mounting procedure can begin. These additional inches give a breather between the edges of the embroidery and the edges of the frame. To mount, for example, "Hawaii One" (⅞" margins required), follow this basic procedure:

1. On one side of artwork, locate very edge of design. Measure ⅞" (this number changes) beyond this point. Mark cloth with pin. On three remaining sides of embroidery, measure ⅞" (this number changes) from edges of design. Mark cloth with pins.
2. With knotted single strand of thread, connect and hand-stitch these lines by following one row in Aida and by weaving in and out cloth with ½" running stitches. These stitched lines are now new edges of your needlework.

3. Measure length and width of this newly stitched shape (Illus. 126).
4. Cut three pieces of mat board, each measuring dimensions in Step 3. Stack them together. Tape in north-south-east-west position (Illus. 127).
5. Cut one piece polyester batting, measuring dimensions in Step 3. Lay batting over boards. Tape as above.
6. Cut one piece of muslin to serve as lining behind needlework. To do, take measurements in Step 3. To these dimensions add 2" seam allowances on all four sides. Cut muslin same size.
7. With right sides up, center muslin over batting/mat board. On back stretch and fold in top and bottom. Tape. Stretch and fold in sides. Tape (Illus. 128).
8. With right sides down, lay embroidery flat. Lay muslin/batting/mat board on top and within stitched edges of design. Stretch and fold in top and bottom. Tape. Stretch and fold in sides. Tape. Get corners neat and flat.
9. On back of design, sew four corners flat with ½" running stitches. Use crewel needle and all six-strands of floss. If necessary use pliers to pull needle through cloth.
10. While still on back, lace back and forth between edges of top and bottom. At same time also work from one side of mat board towards other. Cut floss into two yard lengths. Insert needle 3/16" beyond finished off edges of Aida (Illus. 129). As you approach end of each thread, tighten up floss. Check to see that edge of design lines rest on edges of mat board. Check also to see that needlework is centered, flat, and slightly taut.
11. As in Step 10, lace in opposite direction (Illus. 130).
12. Remove tape and edge of design threads.

Illus. 126.

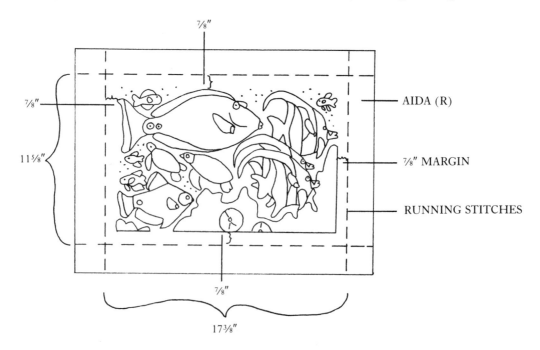

⅞"

⅞"

AIDA (R)

⅞" MARGIN

RUNNING STITCHES

11⅝"

⅞"

17⅜"

3 MAT BOARDS

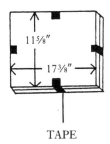

11⅝″

17⅜″

TAPE

VIEW OF BACK

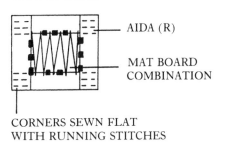

AIDA (R)

MAT BOARD
COMBINATION

CORNERS SEWN FLAT
WITH RUNNING STITCHES

VIEW OF BACK

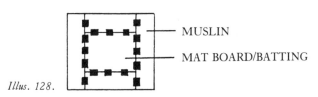

MUSLIN

MAT BOARD/BATTING

Illus. 128.

VIEW OF BACK

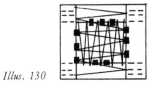

Illus. 130

13. Add frame. Glass is not necessary.

14. Avoid hanging stitchery in direct sunlight (colors fade), near working fireplace (soot), or directly under ceiling vents (dust). Dust picture and frame, occasionally, with soft clean rag.

Metric Equivalents

INCHES TO MILLIMETRES AND CENTIMETRES

MM—millimetres   CM—centimetres

Inches	MM	CM	Inches	CM	Inches	CM
⅛	3	0.3	9	22.9	30	76.2
¼	6	0.6	10	25.4	31	78.7
⅜	10	1.0	11	27.9	32	81.3
½	13	1.3	12	30.5	33	83.8
⅝	16	1.6	13	33.0	34	86.4
¾	19	1.9	14	35.6	35	88.9
⅞	22	2.2	15	38.1	36	91.4
1	25	2.5	16	40.6	37	94.0
1¼	32	3.2	17	43.2	38	96.5
1½	38	3.8	18	45.7	39	99.1
1¾	44	4.4	19	48.3	40	101.6
2	51	5.1	20	50.8	41	104.1
2½	64	6.4	21	53.3	42	106.7
2	76	7.6	22	55.9	43	109.2
3½	89	8.9	23	58.4	44	111.8
4	102	10.2	24	61.0	45	114.3
4½	114	11.4	25	63.5	46	116.8
5	127	12.7	26	66.0	47	119.4
6	152	15.2	27	68.6	48	121.9
7	178	17.8	28	71.1	49	124.5
8	203	20.3	29	73.7	50	127.0

INDEX